Volume XIII, Number 2

Significant Issues Series

The Aspin Papers: Sanctions, Diplomacy, and War in the Persian Gulf

by Representative Les Aspin

foreword by Stanton H. Burnett

The Center for Strategic and International Studies
Washington, D.C.

Library of Congress Cataloging-in-Publication Data

Aspin, Les.
  The Aspin papers: sanctions, diplomacy, and war in the Persian
Gulf / by Les Aspin : foreword by Stanton H. Burnett
    p. cm.—(Significant issues series, ISSN 0736-7136 : v. 13, no. 2)
    ISBN 0-89206-166-9
    1. Iraq-Kuwait Crisis, 1990– 2. United States—Foreign relations—
1989– 3. Geopolitics—Persian Gulf Region. I. Title. II. Series.
DS79.72.A84   1991
956.704′3—dc20   91-7361
                                                                              CIP

The Center for Strategic and International Studies (CSIS), founded in 1962, is an independent, tax-exempt, public policy research institution based in Washington, D.C.

The mission of the Center is to advance the understanding of emerging world issues in the areas of international security, economics, politics, and governance. Through a worldwide capital-to-capital network, it provides decision makers with a strategic perspective that is integrative in nature, comprehensive in scope, anticipatory in its timing, and bipartisan in its approach.

Contents

About the Author

Representative Les Aspin, (D–Wis.) was first elected to the U.S. House of Representatives in 1970. As chairman of the House Armed Services Committee since 1985, Representative Aspin has become one of the foremost leaders on U.S. defense policy. Aspin's vast knowledge and intellectual approach to making policy have earned him wide respect among his colleagues and throughout the nation and the world. His tenure in the House includes positions on the Government Operations (1975–1980), Budget (1981–1984), and District of Columbia (1973–1975) committees.

Aspin received his undergraduate degree summa cum laude in 1960 from Yale University, where he was a member of Phi Beta Kappa. His master's degree is from Oxford University, and his Ph.D. in economics is from the Massachusetts Institute of Technology. In addition to his formal education, Aspin was commissioned in the U.S. Army under the ROTC program in 1966. Aspin left the army as a captain in 1968, going on to become an assistant professor of economics at Marquette University in Milwaukee, Wisconsin.

Foreword

At the end of 1990, Wisconsin Congressman Les Aspin, chairman of the House Armed Services Committee, held a series of hearings on the gathering storm in the Gulf. The hearings riveted the nation as Aspin reached out to a broad range of scholars and authorities, seriously advancing the national debate.

Chairman Aspin's next step was equally remarkable. He wrote a series of three papers on the crisis that were both rich in their summary of testimony and hard-edged in their conclusions. And, in the middle of this effort, he delivered a landmark summary of his findings and views to a packed house at the Center for Strategic and International Studies. His address was the most dramatic and unusual of all the annual Abshire Lectures.

It was an extraordinary conclusion to a year that had begun very differently.

The first half of 1990 had further consolidated the heartening changes of 1989. East–West tension was receding. A band of free democracies was emerging that stretched south from the Baltic to the shores of the Black Sea. The world's only remaining empire was both crumbling at the edges and collapsing inwardly. Many countries in Latin America, Asia, and even the southern tip of Africa were on the road to political and economic reform. Washington appeared to have a breathing spell, internationally, that was needed for addressing serious challenges at home. But just as the pace slowed in Western capitals with the arrival of August, an Iraqi leader, inspired by dreams of Saladin, pitched the world into a crisis that will mark world affairs (and domestic politics and economics) for years to come.

At stake were regional hegemony, control of the chief energy supply of much of the modern world, and the widespread hope for a new international order.

In the United States, a national security debate had already gotten under way. A battle of books and speeches was being waged with seriousness and long-range vision by the few genuine strategic thinkers at the top reaches of American political life, including, especially, Chairman Aspin, Defense Secretary Dick Cheney, and Senator Sam Nunn. Now this vital debate was forced to take into account the storm in the Gulf and to articulate a vision for what seemed a more complex, unpredictable, and perilous future. Along with what might be lost to budget realities, military thinkers now had to consider what might be lost in the desert. Those who had anticipated only low-intensity conflict in the new world order now contemplated troop movements the size of D-Day for landings the size of Normandy.

Congress asserted its role dramatically. Hearings educated the nation, featuring the best minds in U.S. political and military thought. The winter debates on the floor of the two houses were followed more closely by the media and the public than any within recent memory. In the House of Representatives the intellectual guidance was clearly provided by Chairman Aspin. His thinking framed the debate; his actions contributed significantly to the formation of a coherent and broadly supported national strategy for the Gulf.

Chairman Aspin set out to examine three avenues for resolving the conflict: sanctions, war, and diplomacy.

The first paper, looking at sanctions, came out on the day of the Abshire Lecture. In that paper Chairman Aspin asked whether sanctions were working technically or politically. Technically, the answer was positive. Economist Gary Hufbauer found that the sanctions were having much greater success than any previous ones; the paper calls them an "unprecedented" success . . . technically. But Chairman Aspin could find no sign that they were working politically, achieving the results the United States desired—or that they ever would. The scholarly and intelligence estimates that economic pressure would not work against Saddam, but military pressure might, were given close scrutiny. Chairman Aspin's personal conclusion, delivered the same day at CSIS, was that the length of time required for the political success of the sanctions was longer than the cohesiveness of the anti-Saddam coalition could bear. Nor would sanctions alone accomplish all of the legitimate Western objectives in the Gulf.

A week later, the second paper turned to the issue of diplomacy. (The UN deadline was by then less than three weeks away.) The committee examined three main diplomatic options: the Kuwaiti pay-back (withdrawal, followed by concessions from Kuwait), the treatment of Iraq (assuring good post-pullback treatment of Iraq), and linkage (mainly with an international conference on the Arab–Israeli conflict). It examined what each of these did to Middle East stability and to U.S. standing in the region.

Chairman Aspin concluded that a diplomatic solution was a last-best-chance for a peaceful conclusion, but he noted pitfalls to be avoided, if possible. He said an outcome that included Saddam's survival might be trumpeted as a Saddam victory. And an outcome that did not include Saddam's total compliance with the UN resolutions would reward his aggression and damage U.S. credibility. A satisfactory diplomatic solution would also require holding together the anti-Saddam coalition to contain Iraq in the future.

By the time the final paper, on the military option, was issued, diplomatic hopes were fading rapidly. Chairman Aspin started with two presumed military missions for the anti-Iraq coalition: (1) the liberation of Kuwait and reduction of Iraqi forces there and (2) and the destruction of the Iraqi nuclear, chemical, biological, and missile capability.

Aspin compared the military strength of the Gulf adversaries and concluded that the coalition forces had four key advantages: air power, the ability to fight at night, superior strategic and tactical intelligence, and superior logistics.

But it also confronted some uncertainties. We could not be sure which of the coalition allies would actually join the fight. Second, an Iraqi attack on Israel would risk splitting the coalition, although Chairman Aspin concluded that such an attempt would fail. Third, command and control of any multinational force are always troubled, but Chairman Aspin found the pre–January 15 arrangements "satisfactory." Finally, a successful Iraqi attack on the Saudi oil fields would affect both the West's energy supply and world ecology. But the committee's examination of Iraq's ability to achieve such success led to the chairman's conclusion that that ability is very limited and the likely effect on oil production is insignificant.

This final paper assessed Iraqi military strengths (its ground forces capable of conducting position defense and extensive chemical capability) and weaknesses (its poor air force and its logistics, which are vulnerable to air attack). It concluded that the Iraqi soldier's will to fight may disappear in the face of heavy air attack. The committee heard the analysis of CSIS's Brad Roberts that Iraqi chemical and biological warfare (CBW) capabilities were not very significant militarily and concluded that the missile-delivered chemical "terror weapon" against cities was more dangerous than Iraq's ability to sustain effective short-range chemical operations against opposing troops.

The hearings entered the ongoing debate on how a war should be fought, whether by air power alone or by combined operations including ground forces. CSIS's Edward Luttwak and Johns Hopkins' Eliot Cohen asserted that an air campaign could force the Iraqis out of Kuwait because of the threat to Iraq's strategic targets and infrastructure.

But the November announcement of a massive force buildup suggested to some that the administration had already opted for combined operations. Chairman Aspin, listening to the testimony and probing privately, became convinced that "we will fight a phased campaign in the Persian Gulf," that is, a war that begins with an air campaign in Iraq, shifts to an air campaign against military forces in and near Kuwait, and concludes with the commitment of ground forces. The first phases may provide a test for the advocates of air power alone.

This paper offered both profound analysis of alternative war scenarios and excerpts from key testimony about a Gulf war and its outcome, both long and short term. Chairman Aspin thinks a rapid victory with light to moderate U.S. casualties is likely. He is confident about the participation in the fighting of most of the members of the coalition.

The uncertainty weighing most heavily on the chairman at the end of the hearings and of his three papers is clearly the political risk of war in the Gulf—the long-term effect on the Middle East and U.S. interests there. But those interests are so vital that "they are worth going to war for," even for one who believes, as does Chairman Aspin, that war must be a last resort.

• • •

The David M. Abshire Endowed Lecture Series was dedicated in 1982 to mark the twentieth anniversary of the founding of the Center for Strategic and International Studies and as a special tribute from the Center's friends, supporters, and staff to its cofounder, David M. Abshire. The first of the annual lectures was delivered in March 1983.

The Abshire Lectures have usually been landmark analyses of long-term issues, from global *perestroika* to a 10-year balance sheet on U.S.-European relations by the foreign minister of Belgium. The state of the world in the winter of 1990–1991 did not give us this luxury. Instead, this Abshire Lecture makes a resoundingly important contribution to the debate on a historic crisis.

Chairman Aspin used the occasion to remind the country that we had fallen into the trap of taking the unbelievable and the tenuous for granted. The remarkable coalition assembled by President Bush, allying Arab states and the Soviet Union with Washington against an Arab leader, would have been unimaginable a few months earlier and would not endure easily and naturally. Chairman Aspin's sophisticated balancing of cultural and political factors and the careful assessment, based on his first paper, of what international sanctions might not be able to accomplish was the introduction to necessary hard reasoning about the use of force.

This Abshire Lecture and the three papers that accompany it were a tough-minded addition to a fast-moving debate at a moment of crisis. But they are ennobled by the weight of their long-term perspective and the quality of intellect behind them. Historians writing the account of this dangerous winter will pause here.

Stanton H. Burnett
Director of Studies, CSIS
January 1991

Sanctions and Diplomacy in the Persian Gulf Crisis

David M. Abshire Lecture

December 21, 1990

It is a privilege today to give this year's David M. Abshire Lecture. The lectures are a continuing tribute to the founder of CSIS, a dedicated public servant, and a friend. Ambassador Abshire's career stretches from West Point and combat in Korea to service as an assistant secretary of state and ambassador to NATO. He's helped define thoughtful statesmanship in Washington, which is something we can always use.

My topic is the Iraqi invasion of Kuwait and its implications. In a way, that's risky. There is no question but that we are addressing a moving target. In the next few weeks, we are likely to see a great deal of movement. I'd rather not deliver an Abshire lecture in the morning only to have it rendered inoperable by the evening newscasts. In fact, a paragraph in this speech written several days ago will have to be adjusted in the light of what is in the paper this morning.

But I believe there are no more important questions before us today than those presented by this crisis in the Persian Gulf, so here we go.

For the region, this is a watershed event. Things are not likely to be the same again. For example, it's unlikely that Pan-Arab nationalism will ever be quite the same. The U.S.-Saudi relationship has acquired a new visibility. U.S. troops are flooding into Saudi Arabia, which formerly preferred our presence just over the horizon. Egypt and Syria are side by side, not toe to toe. There are strains, perhaps differences, in the U.S.-Israeli relationship. The Middle East is not going to be the same.

Beyond the regional issues, this crisis is the first—maybe the proto-type—crisis of the post–cold war world. How the crisis is resolved—or how the resolution is perceived—will determine a great deal about how American foreign policy is conducted in this new era.

I suspect the lessons learned in this crisis will be cited for years to come when questions arise about whether we can or should work with the United Nations, when questions arise about whether we can or should use force, when questions arise about how Congress can or should use its decision-making power on matters of war and peace.

Of course, it will be much easier to pontificate about all this at next year's Abshire lecture, but I am risking it today because these issues are so important.

The invasion of Kuwait on August 2 confronted the U.S. government with three concerns. In three words, they were oil, aggression, and nukes.

We are sending our men and women in uniform into harm's way and conducting an embargo because Saddam Hussein threatens access to oil and thereby the economic well-being not only of the United States but of all the industrialized countries.

His aggressiveness against a smaller, weaker neighbor is destabilizing and sets a very bad precedent for the new post-cold war world.

And by "nukes" I mean the continuing military threat he poses with his million-man army, biological and chemical weapons, and potential nuclear capability.

The U.S. government has essentially three ways to deal with the crisis: diplomacy, sanctions, and war.

The House Armed Services Committee has undertaken a series of hearings over the last three weeks to explore the costs, risks, advantages, and disadvantages of pursuing each of these three concerns. We have attempted a systematic, thorough examination of each in hopes of helping to provide a basis for Congress and the country to reach a judgment about a proper course of action. Today, in conjunction with this speech, I am releasing a White Paper on sanctions that grows out of this effort. Other reports will follow soon on diplomacy and on how we might prosecute a war in the Persian Gulf. Next week, the White Paper on diplomatic solutions will be released.

Some conclusions on these three options we reached very quickly. One is that the three are interactive. Diplomacy is unlikely to work without a credible military threat; the military threat is enhanced when sanctions constrict the flow of spare parts to Saddam's war machine; and so on. Another conclusion is that there is no one good solution. All have their downsides and there are risks and costs associated with each. Our search is for the best of a bad lot.

Before I discuss the options individually, let me set the military and political context for the discussion.

There has been, I believe, a great deal of agreement on our policy in the Gulf, much more than you might think from following the hearings and the debates in Congress. There was of course a great deal of support for the action taken by the president early in the crisis:

Sending the troops into Saudi Arabia to protect the Saudi Arabian government and oil fields, getting the UN to endorse the sanctions, and getting the UN to endorse using force to backup the sanctions. There is also a great deal of agreement that Saddam Hussein must get out of Kuwait and—if all else fails—I believe there is support for the use of force.

But that qualifier—if all else fails—is very important. It's an issue that will be decided by the calendar—have we given peaceful means enough time to work?

Here's how I believe the Bush administration is dealing with the calendar. Sometime towards the end of October, I believe the administration made the decision that it wanted to bring matters in the Gulf to a head by late winter.

Exhibit A was the announcement on November 8 of a doubling of U.S. troop strength in the Persian Gulf. An increase of about two divisions had been expected. Instead, the announcement was for the equivalent of nearly five divisions.

Exhibit B was the word that there would be no rotation of U.S. troops. The five division equivalents announced November 8 weren't replacements, they were reinforcements.

Exhibit C was the successful initiative to get a UN resolution authorizing the use of force to oust Iraq from Kuwait after January 15, if necessary.

The troop increase, the absence of a troop rotation policy, and the UN deadline engineered by Washington all pointed to a decision by the administration to bring matters to a head somewhere around February.

This was clearly a lot sooner than many members of Congress were prepared for. There had been no explicit discussion of this quickened pace in any of the meetings that were held between the congressional leadership and the White House. In fact, 10 days before the November 8 announcement, there was a meeting in the White House with the congressional leadership at which no mention was made of changing time lines and increasing in troop strength with no rotation policy.

The president and members of his administration repeatedly say they want to work with Congress and are "consulting closely" with us. And there have been meetings, lots of them. The problem hasn't been the quantity of consultations, but the quality.

The November 8 announcement exposed the fault line in what had appeared to be generally solid support for the president's Persian Gulf policies. Many in Congress and elsewhere had assumed that the sanctions option would be given more time to work. The Bush administration was serving notice that that wasn't the case.

Now this sort of thing, of course, is what drives Congress absolutely crazy. The administration, without proper consultation, embarks on a policy that commits the country internationally. Some in Congress have reservations about that policy, but at the same time, it's clear that to force the administration to back off that policy has grave implications. This creates some very strong frustrations on Capitol Hill, and the administration is gambling that those frustration won't come back to bite them.

So the stage is set for a clash over time lines for war and sanctions. In the meantime, however, the stepchild option, diplomacy, has come up on our radar screens.

Ever since the president announced reciprocal visits of Secretary Baker and Iraqi Foreign Minister Tariq Aziz, people have been talking about a negotiated settlement to the crisis. Before we look at other options, let us examine the fresh case for diplomacy.

The administration, of course, denies that negotiations are intended at all. The president says he merely wants to make sure that his get-out-of-Kuwait message gets to Saddam Hussein directly and is not filtered out by sycophantic advisers.

But to the outside observer, it certainly appears that negotiations are going on. Not quietly, but very publicly. First, Secretary Baker says on a Sunday talk show that if Saddam Hussein pulls out of Kuwait, the United States has no interest in attacking Iraq. Next, Saddam Hussein releases all the hostages, thereby removing a flash point. Next, the U.S. government announces it is no longer necessary to keep the U.S. embassy in Kuwait open, removing another flash point. This is not a negligible record for a non-negotiation.

In fact, it has raised the possibility of a diplomatic solution to the crisis.

What kind of resolution might we negotiate? Clearly, Secretary Baker could not agree to anything less than full compliance with the UN resolutions. In the first place, he's not authorized to negotiate on the UN resolutions, and in the second, he has said over and over again that anything else was out of the question. But discussions on other things are possible.

Let us recall the Cuban missile crisis. It was resolved with the withdrawal of Soviet missiles from Cuba—and scored as a major success for President Kennedy. One of the things he did at the time was agree not do something he wouldn't have done anyway—namely, invade Cuba. Jim Baker has already said that if Saddam Hussein pulls out of Kuwait, we would not attack Iraq. This might offer a model for other things we might agree to not do. Something along this line might be enough to get Saddam to withdraw.

Second, like the Cuban missile crisis, we might agree to do something after the crisis that we intended to do anyway—the equivalent of pulling American Jupiter missiles out of Turkey. We might, for example, agree to a peace conference to discuss the Israeli–Arab–Palestinian issue. Or we might agree, as we already have, to negotiations between Iraq and Kuwait about the border after an Iraqi withdrawal.

If those kinds of solutions occurred, then, I think the U.S. government and George Bush could claim victory over the aggressor, and that would be a substantial achievement.

Now this is not an ideal solution. There are those would say with some justification that Saddam Hussein will just go back to brood in his tent in Baghdad for three or four or five years to emerge again, this time with nuclear weapons. In short, they would say we've not only postponed the inevitable, we've made it tougher.

Clearly, the diplomatic option does not deal with the questions of the military threat posed by Iraq and of safeguarding oil supplies. These would have to be dealt with by ancillary measures such as controls on nuclear technologies, an embargo on certain military items, and a continuing multinational armed force of some kind in Kuwait.

But this kind of solution would deal with the immediate aggression. And it was this issue, the invasion of Kuwait, with which the UN resolutions are chiefly occupied. This aggression is the problem that is most effectively dealt with by the stated goals of President Bush's policy. And aggression is the issue that the Bush administration has most publicly and most effectively gone after.

Basically, I believe a negotiated settlement along these lines, provided it included full compliance with the UN resolutions, would be perceived by Americans as a victory for U.S. policy and one that was achieved without bloodshed. I, myself, believe that there is a fair chance that this is how this whole thing will end.

There is another possible outcome that is related. That is a partial Iraqi withdrawal from Kuwait with continued occupation of the Bubiyan and Warbah Islands and the Rumaila oil field. Jim Baker could not and would not agree to that, of course, and so it is not really a negotiated outcome. But it has always been a possibility, and the possibility will be even greater in the next few weeks that Saddam Hussein will simply unilaterally withdraw partially from Kuwait and present us with a fait accompli.

If Saddam Hussein does this, we are left with the question of what the United States and the Allies would do next. This is clearly not an outcome that can be accepted. But in terms of American public opinion, it will be difficult to see how the American people would believe that war was still necessary. This has not been called the "nightmare scenario" for nothing.

If no diplomatic settlement is achieved in the next few weeks, and if we don't have a nightmare, we are left with the conflict in time lines between bringing it all to a head on the one hand, and sanctions on the other.

At the House Armed Services Committee, we've spent a great deal of time and effort trying to understand the issues associated with sanctions. I've learned much from these hearings, which forms the basis for my White Paper on Sanctions. I'm releasing that paper today in conjunction with my speech. It presents my findings in much greater detail. Let me give you the conclusions.

Technically, the sanctions against Iraq are an unprecedented success. Two things chiefly account for this. One is the international unity displayed so far against Iraq's aggression. The second and more important factor is the peculiar geographic vulnerability of Iraq and its enormous dependence on oil exports.

Iraq has only three ways to export oil: by pipeline through Turkey, by pipeline through Saudi Arabia, and by ship down the Persian Gulf. Cutting off these three avenues of export—which we've done—shuts down 95 to 97 percent of Iraq's exports of oil and its only real source of foreign exchange. It almost doesn't matter whether the embargo works to shut off imports into Iraq. Iraq has no foreign exchange to buy those imports and not too many people are going to be selling to Iraq on credit.

The results have been really quite spectacular. According to most estimates, the impact on Iraq will be equal to 48 percent of its gross national product (GNP) over the next one to two years. By contrast, a study of past sanctions campaigns, conducted by the Institute for International Economics, notes that the impact on GNP of successful sanctions campaigns against other targets was more like 2.4 percent.

But it is one thing for sanctions to work technically and it is another thing for them to work politically. Technically they may turn Iraq's economy into a basket case, but they only work politically if they either force the government to change its policy or if the pain of the sanctions forces the Iraqis to change their government.

They have not done so to date, and that's hardly surprising. The real questions are, will they work politically at some time in the future, and can we keep the pressure on until they do? The fact that sanctions are working so well technically means we have to answer these questions very carefully.

Experts on sanctions will tell us that the history of these tools is not very promising. Historically, only one in three such campaigns is successful and that only after four to five years. But they also tell us that the international embargo against Iraq is unique. The extent of the sanctions, the economic impact of these sanctions, the number of countries involved—all make this a case that falls beyond their experience. When all is said and done, they believe that if we keep the corresponding political and military pressure on, the extensive sanctions imposed on Iraq could work a political change in one to two years from their inception. This is about the same time line that the administration's critics would like to give the sanctions to work.

Clearly, there are a number of advantages to allowing the sanctions time to work. First, it avoids war with its terrible loss of life and its uncertain implications for U.S. interests in the region.

Second, it allows for the building of a domestic consensus. In short, it supports a "tried everything" view. Most Americans before they go to war want to be sure that we have tried everything short of war. In this sense, how long we wait for the sanctions to work is really more of a political question than an economic one. But surely the administration's critics have a point here. Waiting until February for the sanctions to work is probably not long enough.

A third argument for giving the sanctions a chance is the impact on the Iraqi military. The CIA believes that the sanctions will begin to have some impact on the Iraqi air force at the end of three months, even without war, because of its reliance on high-tech equipment and on the ground forces in about nine months from now. The intelligence agencies note, however, that Iraq's large numbers of weapons may allow it to avoid some parts shortage though cannibalizing its equipment.

Those are the basic advantages. There are also disadvantages. We can group these under four headings: One, the vulnerability of the coalition; two, the vagaries of international events; three, the clash of cultures; and four, the momentum of choices already made.

First, the vulnerability of the coalition. One of the hallmarks of this time of high-velocity change is that we tend to treat as commonplace today what seemed nearly miraculous yesterday. It is much too soon to take for granted this unlikely grouping of allies in the Persian Gulf.

The brutal invasion and pillaging of a small Arab state by a larger one that also happens to be the best-armed bully on the block is about the only thing that could bring such a coalition together. There are lots of things that could tear it apart, including things that have nothing to do with Kuwait and Iraq.

The incident at the Temple Mount is an example. It had no direct connection to the Persian Gulf crisis, yet it was linked in a very real sense. Can coalition members continue to exert the necessary political, economic, and military pressure on Saddam Hussein in support of the UN sanctions while fighting in New York at the UN over other issues such as resolutions critical of Israel? The answer is yes for today. Tomorrow, we don't know.

The coalition has economic as well as political vulnerabilities. In the United States, we've felt the crisis at the gas pump. The jump in oil prices has pinched us a bit, perhaps worsened our already poor economic performance. But while we feel a pinch, some of our coalition partners are having the daylights squeezed out of them.

For Turkey, Egypt, and other countries in the region, sanctions are definitely a two-edged weapon. The economic impact of the embargo has been severe through loss of trade, remittances from overseas workers, and so on. It is true the oil-rich states of the Gulf can help make up the shortfall, but that money is not likely to filter down to the average person who lost a job because of the sanctions.

Second, there are the vagaries of international events. Will the Syrians and Egyptians, to say nothing of the British, French, and others, be willing to keep their troops there a year to 18 months waiting for the sanctions to work? Or will they fall out over some issue having to do with Israel, or be diverted by another crisis that will require that they deploy their troops elsewhere?

And what of our new-found Middle East ally, the Soviet Union? Only a short time ago, the behavior we are seeing on the part of Moscow would have been the stuff of hallucinations. This is another nearly miraculous turn of events we seem to be taking for granted. Suppose Mr. Gorbachev is replaced by somebody who does not have Mr. Shevardnadze as his foreign minister? Can we be sure that the successor Soviet government will continue to back our hand, or might it revert to a more traditional Soviet attitude toward Iraq?

Third is the clash of cultures. We are building toward an enormous presence in a desert state that is a thinly populated, archly conservative Muslim monarchy. Islamic fundamentalists are already spreading the alarm about the overwhelming presence of westerners in the land that holds the holiest places of Islam.

And the cultures clash both ways, incidentally. In the United States, we can already see the first evidence of resentment at the lengths we are going to be mindful of Saudi sensibilities. I'm not talking about the absence of beer or *Playboy* magazines. I'm talking about reports that Christian and Jewish religious life for our men and women of Desert Shield is officially muted lest it offend our hosts. Whatever the facts, such reports can only irritate an American public that believes those same men and women may lose their lives to pull Saudi chestnuts out of the fire. The Saudi treatment of women is another issue on which we will have little sympathy.

Finally, there is the momentum of choices already made. Whether rightly or wrongly, the Bush administration has embarked on a course of action likely to bring this crisis to a head, and it has brought the military alliance along with it. The administration time line runs to February and it's there for everyone to see, including Saddam Hussein. For the administration's critics in Congress and elsewhere, an attempt to walk the administration back down that time line cannot be undertaken lightly.

First, there is the enormous problem of dealing with a U.S. troop strength of more than 400,000 in Saudi Arabia for an extended period of time. I don't believe, as some have claimed, that troops can sit in the desert for a year or more and maintain anything like their peak combat effectiveness.

That means we would need a rotation policy of some kind. At a troop level that high, it would involve partial mobilization of the reserves, substitution of units of one service by units of another service, and maybe developing some special units that do not exist in large enough numbers to rotate. A very tough problem.

But second, success at walking the administration back down its time line could spell failure in the crisis. It could send a very dangerous message to Saddam Hussein and probably to the world. The administration has brought the coalition along on its time line. They have, in effect, decided that January 15 is as long as they'll wait to see if the sanctions work. Having once given the signal that we are heading for a showdown sometime in late winter, we'd have to calculate carefully what it would cost to switch signals.

I would argue that maintaining our credibility now is more important if we hope not to go to war than it would be if we planned today to blast Saddam out of Kuwait. Here's why. If we hope that some combination of sanctions, diplomacy, and threat of war will force him out of Kuwait, then that threat of war must be credible. Even the sanctions experts—the ones who are most optimistic about how sanctions might work—all believe that it is not just sanctions but a combination of economic pressure with political, military, and psychological pressure.

What constitutes a credible military threat, how we might prosecute a war, and the necessity of allied participation are topics I plan to deal with in another speech. I'll also deal with the question of how Congress should fulfill its constitutional role—and Congress must have a role if the administration plans to go to war.

But in the meantime, this examination of sanctions and diplomacy leads to important conclusions.

First, I believe that the interests we have at stake in the Persian Gulf are vital. If all else fails, they are worth going to war for.

Second, I come to the conclusion that relying on sanctions is not the answer. Technically, they are working superbly—really to an unprecedented degree. Whether they can be made to work politically is more problematical. Pain for the Iraqi people is not the same thing as pain for Saddam Hussein. Keeping up the requisite political, military, and psychological pressure is a major stumbling block. Can we keep the alliance together and focused—especially focused—long enough for the sanctions to work politically? I judge the probability of that to be very low.

Third, I judge the possibility of a diplomatic solution to be more promising. Some will not be happy with this conclusion, but I believe the test of a diplomatic solution is the extent of the compliance with the UN resolutions. A complete withdrawal by Saddam Hussein from Kuwait will be a victory almost regardless of what else is agreed upon around the edges. A partial withdrawal is only a partial victory.

Finally, we must mean what we say when we deal with the Saddam Husseins of the world. If the United States is to be credible in the post–cold war world, if the United Nations is to be a useful vehicle for collective security, then we cannot shrink from the use of force. A future aggressor can ignore the UN's next deadline if we ignore this one.

Thank you.

The Role of Sanctions in Securing U.S. Interests in the Persian Gulf

December 21, 1990

Introduction

Hearings and Purpose of Report

On December 4, 1990, the House Armed Services Committee began a series of hearings on the Persian Gulf Crisis. Their purpose was to provide a systematic, thorough examination of the three main avenues for resolution of the conflict: sanctions, war, and diplomacy. The committee examined the costs and risks of each, what chance each option had of succeeding, and what success might mean in each case.

During the first week of hearings, the committee dealt with sanctions. Dr. Phebe Marr from the National Defense University, former Ambassador to Saudi Arabia James Akins, and Dr. Judith Kipper—all three Iraqi specialists—and the former director of the CIA's office for psychological profiles, Dr. Jerrold Post, discussed how susceptible Saddam Hussein and his regime would be to the pressure of sanctions. CIA Director William Webster gave an unclassified statement, followed by a discussion in closed session, on how the sanctions were working against Iraq.

Several experts on Iraq's nuclear, biological, and chemical capabilities—the Carnegie Endowment's Leonard S. Spector, Brad Roberts from CSIS, and the Brookings Institution's Janne Nolan—described the status of Iraq's programs for mass-destruction weapons and delivery systems and analyzed the impact that sanctions would have upon them. Finally, James A. Bill from the College of William and Mary, Martin Indyk of the Washington Center for Near East Policy, and former NSC adviser William Quandt assessed the regional impact of a solution arrived at primarily through the pressure for sanctions.

This White Paper summarizes what I have drawn from these hearings and other sources on the sanctions option. It is my report and not that of the House Committee on Armed Services. I offer it in hope of contributing to the substantive debate on the issues raised by the Persian Gulf crisis.

My analysis of the sanctions option will address several key questions: what they can achieve, how might they be made to work, whether they can be sustained long enough to work and at what cost, and what are the implications of a solution arrived at by sanctions. It is intended to help provide Congress the information it needs to carry out its constitutional responsibility.

U.S. Interests and Objectives

The invasion of Kuwait on August 2 confronted the U.S. government with three concerns. In three words, they were oil, aggression, and nukes.

The crisis in the Persian Gulf threatens the fundamental and long-standing interest of the United States in maintaining regional stability in the Middle East. Iraq invaded and occupied Kuwait just as the cold war was ending. The rules that will govern the new world order are being fashioned in the crucible of this crisis. Saddam Hussein should not be allowed to enjoy the fruits of his aggression if we are to create a new, peaceful international order for the post–cold war era.

Rewarding aggression usually encourages more aggression, both from Saddam and other would-be Saddams. Thus, it is in our interest that the principle that aggression does not pay be reinforced by the resolution of this crisis. Otherwise, we face greater problems in the future.

Every president since Franklin D. Roosevelt has committed the United States to the pursuit of security and stability in the Persian Gulf. In part, this reflects our economic interest. The need of the United States and the world for reliable access to oil requires, in the short run, that Saddam Hussein's seizure of Kuwait's oil and attempt to dominate Gulf oil politics be opposed. In the long run, it requires security and stability in the Gulf where over half of the world's known oil reserves are located. Our pursuit of stability in the Gulf also stems from our concern about the security of important long-term allies and our general interest in stability as a prerequisite for economic growth and democracy.

Saddam Hussein's aggressiveness against a smaller, weaker neighbor destabilized the region. His million-man army, biological and chemical weapons, and coming nuclear capability pose a long-term threat to the region. Iraq's military leverage in the region must be neutralized if security and stability are to be achieved in the Persian Gulf.

As a matter of national policy, the United States is committed to the defense of Saudi Arabia and the UN approved goals of ousting Iraq from Kuwait, restoring the Kuwaiti government, and freeing foreign nationals. This set of objectives, even though it does not address all of the U.S. interests at stake, has evolved as the bottom line for President Bush and most members of Congress and is often used as the litmus test for evaluating policy alternatives. A principal criterion for evaluating an option in the Gulf must be whether it accomplishes the UN objectives—that is, Iraq's unconditional and complete withdrawal from Kuwait and the restoration of the Kuwaiti government, now that the hostages have been released.

There are principally three means for achieving U.S. objectives in the Gulf—sanctions, the threat and use of military force, and diplomacy. None of them work in isolation. A solution arrived at by sanctions or the threat of military action will have a diplomatic end-game. We can examine the implications of a settlement reached primarily through each of the options at our disposal, however. In the case of sanctions, we need to look at what might be achieved through the use of sanctions alone, as well as sanctions buttressed by a credible military threat.

Are the Sanctions Working?

There are two main aspects to this question:
- How well are sanctions working technically?
- Are they achieving their political purposes?

Sanctions work technically if they shut down Iraq's trade, squeeze its economy, and impose hardship on its people.

Sanctions work politically only if they induce Iraq to withdraw from Kuwait. This could happen in two ways. They could force Saddam Hussein to withdraw from Kuwait, or they could cause Saddam's overthrow and his replacement by a government willing to withdraw.

Sanctions are an Unprecedented Technical Success

The embargo on Iraq's trade is essentially total. Director of Central Intelligence Judge William Webster told the committee that sanctions have shut off more than 90 percent of imports and more than 97 percent of exports. The embargo has deprived Saddam Hussein of roughly $1.5 billion of foreign exchange earnings monthly, equivalent by itself to more than a third of Iraq's total national product. Iraqi international financial holdings and credit have been frozen, and Iraq has no access to Kuwaiti resources held abroad.

Iraq's economy appears to be unusually vulnerable to such a total trade embargo. Iraq is extremely dependent on one commodity, oil, for 95 percent of its exports. Iraq is also import-dependent with 30 percent of its GNP consisting of imports. Iraq imported an extremely high fraction of its food—as much as two-thirds of its calories, over 70 percent of its grain consumption, and over 90 percent of its sugar and vegetable oils. By contrast, Japan, a nation extremely sensitive to its high import dependence, imported the equivalent of 10 percent of its GNP and less than 50 percent of its food. As James A. Placke, a Middle Eastern economic specialist formerly in the U.S. State Department, argued before the Senate:

> The Iraqi economy . . . is exceedingly dependent upon a single natural resource, petroleum, with an inefficient and resource-deprived—but potentially significant—agricultural sector and an industrial sector skewed toward defense-related production. As a consequence, Iraq is uniquely vulnerable . . . to the effects of a trade embargo because of its dependence on foreign sources for higher quality consumer goods—including foodstuffs—but especially for a wide array of industrial materials, semi-finished goods, technical services, and supplies.

Iraq clearly was surprised by the international response that followed its invasion of Kuwait. There is no evidence that Iraq deliberately stocked up on crucial supplies or spare parts, whether military or civilian, before its invasion of Kuwait. Prior to the invasion, Iraq relied extensively on imports of foreign technology including spare parts and also on foreign engineers. Those familiar with Iraqi industry believe that the embargo, together with the departure of foreign specialists, has already set back Iraq's industrialization a decade.

Iraq is a relatively advanced country by third world standards, with a substantial middle class conditioned to expect material progress. The population is 70 percent urban. As recently as 1987 Iraq had a severe labor shortage, and unemployment in 1989 was estimated at under 5 percent. The real growth rate last year was 5 percent. After nearly a decade of war Iraq's GNP per capita last year was nearly 50 percent greater than Turkey's.

Government expenditures exceeded one-half of the GNP of $35 billion. Revenues from oil exports approximated two-thirds of the government expenditures and were about equal in size to imports. With revenues from oil exports as well as imports cut off, the government will be severely restricted in its ability to provide benefits and services to its population. The phrase "command economy" will take on a new meaning.

CIA Director William Webster provided the committee the following assessment of the economic impact of sanctions to date:

> The price of sugar has risen from $32 to over $580 a 50 kilogram bag, [even with the prices calculated at a constant official exchange rate]. Baghdad remains concerned about its food stocks and continues to try to extend stocks and, increasingly, to divert supplies to the military. In late November, Baghdad cut civilian rations for the second time since the rationing program began while announcing increases in rations for military personnel and their families.
>
> Many industries have already shut down . . . including many light industrial and assembly plants as well as the country's only tire-manufacturing plant. In addition, services ranging from medical care to sanitation have been curtailed. . . . Despite these shutdowns, the most vital industries—including electric power generation and refining—do not appear threatened.

There has already been large-scale labor dislocation, especially in the petroleum industry. The unemployed so far have been absorbed into the lower skill jobs, formerly held by departing foreign workers, and into the army.

Judge Webster testified that the sanctions will soon have an even greater impact on the life of the Iraqi people:

> The autumn harvest and the seizure of stocks from Kuwait have provided a temporary increase in the variety of food available to the Iraqi people. By next spring, Iraqis will have made major changes in their diets. Poultry, a staple of the Iraqi diet, will not be available. Unless Iraq receives humanitarian food aid or unless smuggling increases, some critical commodities such as sugar and edible oils will be in short supply. Distribution problems are likely to create localized shortages. . . . We expect that Baghdad will be able to maintain grain consumption—mainly wheat, barley, and rice—at about two-thirds of last year's level until the next harvest in May.
>
> The spring grain and vegetable harvest will again augment food stocks, although only temporarily . . . . Iraq does not have the ability

to become self-sufficient in food production over the next year. . . . Even if . . . the weather . . . is good, Iraqis will be able to produce less than half the grain they need. In addition, Iraq's vegetable production next year may be less than normal because of its inability to obtain seed stock from abroad. Iraq had obtained seed from the United States, the Netherlands, and France.

At current rates of depletion, we estimate Iraq will have nearly depleted its available foreign exchange reserves by next Spring, leaving it little cash with which to entice potential sanctions-busters. Able to obtain even fewer key imports, Iraq's economic problems will begin to multiply as Baghdad is forced to gradually shut down growing numbers of facilities in order to keep critical activities functioning as long as possible. Economic conditions will be noticeably worse, and Baghdad will find allocating scarce resources a significantly more difficult task.

Professor Gary Hufbauer of Georgetown University and his colleagues at the Institute for International Economics have surveyed 115 previous cases where sanctions were imposed. Historically, when 50 of the target country's trade was covered by sanctions, there was a 50 percent chance that sanctions would achieve their goals. The current instance covers virtually 100 percent of Iraq's trade, three to four times greater coverage than the average of previous sanctions successes.

Previous successful sanctions episodes cost the target an annual average of only 2.4 percent of its GNP. The most stringent case cost the target country the equivalent of 16 percent of its GNP. In contrast they estimate the welfare of Iraqis will be reduced by an amount equal to 48 percent of Iraq's GNP. This impact will occur quickly in comparison to the amount of time sanctions took to gain their full effect in other cases.

Impact of Sanctions on the Iraqi Military

Iraq has invested heavily in its effort to develop an indigenous armaments industry with some success. Its operations still require foreign experts, foreign inputs, and spare parts for the production equipment, however. Although there is no evidence that Iraq made a special effort to build up its military stocks before the August 2 invasion, Iraq already had large stocks of most general-issue military spares and, except for its most modern systems, can cannibalize much of its equipment outside the Kuwaiti theater to keep its relatively static defense intact.

CIA Director Webster told the committee that sanctions could weaken the Iraqi military machine over time, even though it was currently affecting the Iraqi military only at the margins:

> Iraq's fairly static, defensive posture will reduce wear and tear on military equipment and, as a result, extend the life of its inventory of spare parts and maintenance items. Under non-combat conditions, Iraqi ground and air forces can probably maintain near-current levels of readiness for as long as nine months.
>
> We expect the Iraqi air force to feel the effects of the sanctions more quickly and to a greater degree than the Iraqi ground forces because of its greater reliance on high technology and foreign equipment and technicians. Major repairs to sophisticated aircraft like the [Mirage] F-1 will be achieved with significant difficulty, if at all, because of the exodus of foreign technicians. Iraqi technicians, however, should be able to maintain current levels of aircraft sorties for three to six months.
>
> The Iraqi ground forces are more immune to sanctions. Before the invasion, Baghdad maintained large inventories of basic military supplies, such as ammunition, and supplies probably remain adequate. The embargo will eventually hurt Iraqi armor by preventing the replacement of old fire-control systems and creating shortages of additives for various critical lubricants. Shortages will also affect Iraqi cargo trucks over time.

In contrast to his earlier skepticism concerning the military impact of sanctions, General Colin Powell, chairman of the Joint Chiefs of Staff, told the committee on December 14 that sanctions could weaken Iraq's force over time. General Norman Schwarzkopf, U.S. commander in Saudi Arabia, told a committee delegation to Saudi Arabia much the same thing. They both suggested, however, that the Iraqi army could go into "hibernation" if the military threat against him declined, thus reducing the impact of sanctions on the Iraqi military.

Political Impact of Sanctions

The success of sanctions must ultimately be measured not by the degree of trade restriction or even the degree of pain inflicted on Iraq, but by Iraqi actions that comply with the UN objectives. Saddam has complied with the UN resolutions in only one respect. He has released the hostages. It is not possible to know which of our actions might have influenced him to do so. In addition to the sanctions, the U.S. military buildup was announced on November 8, on November 28 the UN Security Council Resolution authorizing the use of force was passed, and on November 29, President Bush made his offer to exchange visits of foreign ministers. Saddam Hussein has given no other indication that he will comply with the UN demands. Moreover, Saddam continues to deploy forces to Kuwait and fortify his defenses.

There have been no signs of significant internal protest against Saddam's rule, but perhaps this is not surprising in a regime as repressive as Saddam's. There have been no mass desertions among troops in Kuwait. Government-sponsored demonstrations against the United States and the anti-Iraq coalition continue to be staged in Baghdad and other cities, without any unusual security presence.

In October Iraq announced that gasoline rationing would begin, but this order was soon revoked as Saddam replaced the long-time oil minister with his own son-in-law. Gasoline rationing had reportedly been instituted because of the shortage of crucial petroleum additives, which were largely imported. This incident certainly suggests that Saddam is concerned over the domestic impact of sanctions, which could be an early sign that sanctions were having a political effect. It could also be the case, however, that Saddam was more concerned with his international image of invulnerability than about his domestic support.

Saddam has also replaced his military chief of staff and his defense minister, but in both cases the replacements are among his most experienced and competent generals. This suggests that Saddam is preparing for war, not acting to preempt political threats to his rule. There have been rumors, but no confirmation, that some generals had been executed for opposing his invasion of Kuwait. These rumors, of course, are endemic in a country whose own government has admitted that there were five coup attempts in the year prior to the invasion of Kuwait, according to former Ambassador to Saudi Arabia Akins.

CIA Director Webster observed, however, that the Iraqi people had experienced much higher levels of hardship than they were currently experiencing and had shown no sign of turning on Saddam. During the Iran–Iraq War, the Iraqis endured "the combination of economic distress, high casualty rates, and repeated missile and air attacks" without "a single significant public disturbance even though casualties hit 2.3 percent of the total Iraqi population—about the same as the percentage of U.S. casualties during the civil war."

But the economic hardship in Iraq will increase. Moreover, the high casualties and sense of danger that the Iraqi people suffered during that war were not accompanied by economic distress. During the Iran–Iraq War, Iraq received a great deal of economic support from the Gulf oil states, particularly Kuwait and Saudi Arabia. While Saddam's ambitious development program slowed, it did not stop. Economic resources were used to assuage the hardships of war. Families of men killed or distinguished in the war were commonly rewarded with new cars. If sanctions remain in place, there will no early material rewards for military sacrifice.

Will the Sanctions Work Politically in the Future?

There are two principal scenarios through which sanctions might succeed: Saddam decides to withdraw, or he is overthrown and his successors withdraw.

In the first scenario, the key is Saddam's own ways of thinking and his information. In the second scenario, the key is the motivation and abilities of those with the physical power to overthrow Saddam.

CIA William Webster publicly addressed both of these issues when he appeared before the committee on December 4. This was his summary judgment:

> Despite mounting disruptions and hardships resulting from sanctions, Saddam apparently believes that he can outlast international resolve to maintain sanctions. We see no indication that Saddam is concerned, at this point, that domestic discontent is growing to levels that may threaten his regime or that problems from the sanctions are causing him to rethink his policy on Kuwait. The Iraqi people have experienced considerable deprivation in the past. Given the brutal nature of the Iraqi security services, the population is not likely to oppose Saddam openly. Our judgment has been, and continues to be, that there is no assurance or guarantee that economic hardships will compel Saddam to change his policies or lead to internal unrest that would threaten his regime.

In short, the CIA concludes that there is no sign yet that sanctions are working politically, and it is far from certain that they ever would work.

This assessment, however, does not include a judgment about what might convince Saddam Hussein to withdraw from Kuwait. Judge Webster addressed this in an interview with the *Washington Post* on December 14. He said that U.S. intelligence experts had concluded that the Iraqi president will not withdraw his troops from Kuwait until convinced he "is in peril of imminent military attack."

Until then, the CIA director said, Saddam will try to stretch out the Gulf crisis, possibly by staging a partial pullout or some other move short of the UN demand for a full withdrawal by January 15. The danger in this, he added, is that the Iraqi leader will continue to believe he can succeed "until the first shell is lobbed over him."

Clearly, it is this intelligence judgment—that economic pressure won't work against Saddam, but military pressure might even though it risks war—that underlies the Bush administration's apparent decision in early November to switch from a policy relying primarily on sanctions to one primarily relying on the threat of war. The committee examined this judgment very closely in its hearings.

Saddam's Susceptibility to Pressure

Three regional specialists and long-time Saddam-watchers—Doctors Marr and Kipper and Ambassador Akins—and Dr. Post, a political psychologist who formerly directed the CIA's office of psychological profiles, appeared before the committee to discuss Saddam Hussein's susceptibility to the pressure of sanctions.

Resolving the crisis in the Persian Gulf probably requires changing the mind of Saddam Hussein. In his *Washington Post* interview, Judge Webster commented on how much events have been personalized:

> "In this particular crisis," Webster said, "so much seems to reside in the head of one man." He said Saddam is "not getting very much advice from anyone or taking much advice from anybody. He has CNN [Cable News Network], he has the newspapers, he has what people are sending him to read, but he has no one there to say, 'Hey, look' . . . . "

Psychologist Dr. Jerrold Post described for the Committee Saddam's isolation, which is reinforced by his brutality:

> While he is psychologically in touch with reality, he is often polit-ically out of touch with reality. Saddam's world view is narrow and distorted, and he has scant experience out of the Arab world.
> . . . He is surrounded by sycophants, who are cowed by Saddam's well founded reputation for brutality and are afraid to contradict him. He has ruthlessly eliminated perceived threats to his power and

equates criticism with disloyalty. At one time early in his presidency, he identified 500 Communist party members for execution and had his senior officials form the execution squads . . . . [In 1982, when the war against Iran was going badly] Saddam asked his ministers to candidly give their advice, and the Minister of Health suggested Saddam temporarily step down, to resume the presidency after peace had been established. Saddam reportedly thanked him for his candor and ordered his arrest. His wife pled for her husband's return. The next day, Saddam returned her husband's body to her in a black canvas bag, chopped into pieces.

Saddam's psychological profile suggests that it is not likely that the economic deprivation of the Iraqi people will convince him to give up Kuwait. Dr. Post described a political personality constellation— "messianic ambition for unlimited power, absence of conscience, unconstrained aggression"—that is extremely "dangerous":

Saddam's pursuit of power for himself and Iraq is boundless. In fact, in his mind, the destiny of Saddam and Iraq are one and indistinguishable. His exalted self concept is fused with his Bathist political ideology. Bathist dreams will be realized when the Arab nation is unified under one strong leader. In Saddam's mind, he is destined for that role . . . . In pursuing his goals, Saddam uses aggression instrumentally. He uses whatever force is necessary, and will, if he deems it expedient, go to extremes of violence, including the use of weapons of mass destruction . . . . While Hussein is not psychotic, he has a strong paranoid orientation. He is ready for retaliation and, not without reason, sees himself as surrounded by enemies. But he ignores his role in creating those enemies, and righteously threatens his targets. The conspiracy theories he spins are not merely for popular consumption in the Arab world, but genuinely reflect his paranoid mindset. He is convinced that the United States, Israel and Iran have been in league for the purpose of eliminating him . . . .

The three regional specialists—Drs. Marr and Kipper and Ambassador Akins—all agreed with this psychological portrait, as did many other witnesses appearing before the committee.

The witnesses also agreed, however, that Saddam would reverse course if he believed his political survival was threatened. Dr. Marr said that she believed that

Saddam will withdraw when his power base, and his political survival, is threatened. He wants to survive, not simply for personal
reasons, but to assure the achievement of his goals and ambitions.
He wants, and intends, to rebuild Iraq and go on to play a major
role in the region. This power base can be threatened in several
ways. Sanctions will erode Saddam's support in the middle class
accustomed to urban amenities it will not be able to get, and in the
military they may see its equipment and technology degraded.
However, in my view, this will be a long, slow process that will be
difficult to detect and possible for Saddam to contain, given his
control over his populace. Support for Saddam, especially among his
armed forces, can also be eroded by a credible military threat which,
while riskier, is likely to end the crisis sooner. Such a threat need
not result in actual military action if handled carefully.

Dr. William Quandt, a former NSC official and Middle Eastern
expert, also sees Saddam as a "survivor" who "if he sees that his
survival is at stake can just as easily turn around and declare victory as
he withdraws from Kuwait." Drs. Marr and Post note that he has done
so on several occasions: in 1975 when he agreed to divide the Shatt
al-Arab with the shah of Iran because of the Kurdish rebellion; in 1982
when he retreated from Iran, calling it a voluntary withdrawal in the
interests of peace, because of disastrous military losses; and in 1990
when he reversed himself again on the Shatt al-Arab, promising to give
back to the Iranians the only thing the Iraqis won in a bitter eight-year
war.
How can Saddam be persuaded that his survival is at stake? Dr.
Post believes that

The only language Saddam Hussein understands is the language of
power. Without this demonstrable willingness to use force, even if
the sanctions are biting deeply, Saddam is quite capable of putting
his population through a sustained period of hardship, as he has in
the past. It is crucial to demonstrate that unless he withdraws, his
career as a world class political actor will be ended.

Ambassador Akins, as well as Drs. Kipper and Post, believes that
Saddam cannot withdraw without some sort of "fig-leaf" to preserve his
honor and dignity. If presented with the stark choice of war or losing
Kuwait, Ambassador Akins asks:

Will this overwhelming force give Saddam second thoughts and cause him to withdraw? Will Saddam accept a humiliating defeat and simply back away? Highly unlikely.

Our other witnesses did not go so far. Dr. Kipper apparently believed that Saddam Hussein has already decided that he must withdraw and that "direct talks with American officials [as offered by President Bush on November 30] may be the face-saving device Saddam Hussein needs to withdraw from Kuwait." Dr. Post, however, puts the "face-saving" issue into a broader context:

> Honor and reputation must be interpreted in an Arab context. Saddam has already achieved considerable honor in the eyes of the Arab masses for having the courage to stand up to the West. It should be remembered that even though Egypt militarily lost the 1973 war with Israel, Sadat became a hero to the Arab world for his willingness to attack—and initially force back—the previously invincible forces of Israel. Qadhafi mounted an air attack when the United States crossed the so-called "line of death." Even though his jets were destroyed in the ensuing conflict, Qadhafi's status was raised in the Arab world. Indeed, he thanked the United States for making him a hero. Thus Saddam can find honor in the present situation. His past history reveals a remarkable capacity to find face saving justification when reversing his course in very difficult circumstances. Nevertheless, it is important not to insist on total capitulation and humiliation, for this could drive Saddam into a corner and make it impossible for him to reverse his course. He will only withdraw from Kuwait if he believes he can survive with his power and his dignity intact.

It was the conclusions of our witnesses that

1. There is little doubt that convincing Saddam himself to withdraw from Kuwait will be very difficult.

2. The economic pressure from sanctions do not affect him directly; they squeeze the Iraqi people, and Saddam has shown himself to be impervious to the suffering of others, working actively and brutally to preempt threats against him.

3. What will compel Saddam to switch course is a threat to his political survival. Sanctions might, but are unlikely to, produce such a threat—the threat of war is more likely to.

Prospects for Saddam's Overthrow

Saddam might be induced to withdraw from Kuwait if he thought that the sanctions were causing forces in Iraq to move against him. As mentioned previously, CIA Director Webster did not report any signs so far that Saddam felt threatened or should feel threatened.

Dr. Kipper flatly asserted that Saddam Hussein is a "ruthless dictator who has an absolute monopoly on power." None of the witnesses appearing before the committee believed that an East European-like peoples' revolt was feasible. Nor did the externally based opposition groups pose any threat to Saddam because they had been ruthlessly repressed inside Iraq.

The most likely source of a coup is the army. According to Dr. Marr, the army, or at least its officer corps, is a middle class institution that will be sensitive to urban living standards and viewpoints and thus might be susceptible to the pressure of sanctions. Saddam Hussein, however, has insulated the army from the economic effects of the sanctions, in part through the distribution of booty taken from Kuwait. Although she believed that a decision by Saddam himself to leave Kuwait was more likely, Dr. Marr believed that

> It is possible, although not probable in my estimation, that if a military threat appears sufficiently serious to jeopardize the cohesion of the state, or to destroy, rather than defeat, the military, that some military leadership could emerge to challenge Saddam's leadership. Such a move could also be made by someone from within the Establishment. However, because the risk of such action is high, and the ability to organize such an attempt so difficult, revolt from within does not have much probability. Moreover, Saddam Husain [sic] is likely to recognize that threat sooner than anyone else and take steps to avoid it either by repressing the move or by withdrawing.

Dr. Marr's analysis suggests that if the military were to move against Saddam it would be for the same reason that might lead Saddam to withdraw, namely, the threat of war. As discussed previously, the sanctions have had little impact on the military so far, although it will begin to weaken in the next three to nine months. Nevertheless, the prospect that sanctions might cause the factions within the army to move against Saddam seems small.

The CIA appears to share Dr. Marr's views and does not believe that Saddam's recent appointment of a new defense minister suggests discontent in the military. Rather, CIA Director Webster told the *Washington Post* that he hoped that Major General Saadi Tuma Abbas, a much decorated war hero for his 1982 defense of Basrah during the Iran-Iraq War, might be able to warn Saddam what he is up against. Judge Webster added, however, that he thought the Iraqi leader was taking the crisis day by day and probably does not know himself "what his decision is going to be."

How Long for Sanctions to Work Politically?

Despite the stringency of the sanctions, specialists on Iraq, as well as the Director of Central Intelligence, have concluded that there is no guarantee that sanctions could force Iraq out of Kuwait by making Saddam retreat or by causing the overthrow of his regime. Several witnesses, however, believed that although there is no guarantee, given a fair test of time, sanctions could work politically. What constitutes a fair test of sanctions?

From their study of sanctions episodes, Kimberly Elliot, Gary Hufbauer, and Jeffrey Schott told the Senate Foreign Relations Committee that "history suggests that one to two years will pass before the sanctions prevail" in the Persian Gulf. Sanctions, they argue, will only have a strong political effect once their staying power has been demonstrated and once they have begun to have a strong impact on civilian consumption or on the readiness of the military forces.

According to the Hufbauer study, it took an average of slightly less than two years from the onset of sanctions, or at most several months after the full economic effects of the sanctions were felt, in those instances in which sanctions successfully achieved major changes in behavior from the target state. In most historical cases, sanctions were imposed more gradually and much less completely than is now the case against Iraq.

Sanctions on Iraq will bite hardest during next August/September— the height of summer in Iraq—and it could be that sanctions might achieve their political objectives at that time. There appears to be a broad consensus among experts that they are not likely to work before then. Many experts, including Drs. Hufbauer and Marr, believe it would take one to two years from when sanctions were first applied in August. A fair test of sanctions, therefore, is probably up to a year or more, but certainly through September of next year.

Advantages and Risks of Relying on Sanctions

Although this White Paper examines whether Saddam can be forced out of Kuwait primarily through the pressure of sanctions, sanctions do not operate in isolation. They are also buttressed at this time by Saddam's diplomatic isolation and the pressure posed by the military forces arrayed against him. In fact, most witnesses believed that the effectiveness of sanctions would depend, in part, upon how much diplomatic and military pressure was maintained against Saddam Hussein.

Advantages

There are three principal advantages of extending reliance on sanctions past January 15. First, it may avoid a war with its high costs, loss of life, and uncertain implications for U.S. interests.

Second, a decision to give sanctions a longer test could attract significant additional support domestically and create a broader consensus if it should become necessary to use force to achieve the UN objectives.

Finally, the continued operation of sanctions will weaken Iraq's military effort. The CIA believes that the sanctions will begin to have some impact on the Iraqi air force at the end of three months and on the ground forces in about nine months. Our forces would suffer fewer casualties should war eventually ensue.

Risks

There are several categories of risk in sustaining a sanction policy over a prolonged period of time.

The first question is whether the coalition against Iraq can be maintained. This is not just a coalition for maintaining the sanctions—the U.S. Navy with the support of Turkey, Saudi Arabia, and, perhaps Iran could bottle up Iraq's oil—but a coalition for bringing the combination of economic, military, and diplomatic pressures that might induce Iraq to withdraw from Kuwait.

It is not "sanctions alone" that will do the job. Elliot, Hufbauer, and Schott assert that "since the sanctions against Iraq were imposed so swiftly, decisively and comprehensively, there is a high probability that—combined with a military threat—they can contribute" to Iraq's compliance with the UN resolutions "in a year or two." So the coalition must be maintained not just for the economic embargo but for the military threat as well. Can this be done for a year or two?

It is an unlikely grouping of allies in the Persian Gulf, brought together only by Saddam's brutal invasion and pillaging of a small neighbor. The idea that the United States, Syria, Iran, and Saudi Arabia would be on the same side would have been unthinkable before August 2.

There are several potential fault lines in this alliance. Most prominent is the strain caused by the U.S. relationship with Israel. The Temple Mount incident, which derailed the U.S. diplomatic effort against Iraq for at least two weeks in the United Nations, illustrates the fragility of the anti-Iraq coalition. Our Arab partners are more closely aligned with Iraq on Israeli issues than they are with the United States.

There is also a clash of cultures. We are building an enormous military presence in a desert state that is a thinly populated, conservative Muslim monarchy. Islamic fundamentalist groups throughout the region initially opposed Saddam's invasion of Kuwait, but this stopped when U.S. troops started to arrive in Saudi Arabia, home and keeper of the most important holy cities of Islam. Now Islamic fundamentalists are spreading the alarm about the presence of Western infidels as Saddam attempts to pose as their leader.

There are also heavy economic burdens being borne by Turkey, Jordan, Egypt, and other countries in the region. The impact has been severe through loss of trade, remittances from overseas workers, and so on. While it is true that these states can be compensated for their losses (see Appendix A for a short status report), this governmental aid is not likely to filter down into the Arab masses, which already support Saddam Hussein's showdown with the West. The potential for political instability will only increase with time.

Can the military option be maintained for the one to two years that Hufbauer et al. believe it will take for sanctions to work? Will the Syrians, French, and Egyptians be willing to keep their troops there? Will the Saudis hold firm or cut a deal with Saddam to reduce the destabilizing presence of over 400,000 Americans?

There is a time of great historical change. The Soviet Union's support in the Security Council has been crucial and would have been unthinkable before Mikhail Gorbachev took power. The shocking resignation on December 20 of Foreign Minister Shevardnadze, certainly the most supportive Soviet official of U.S. policy in the Gulf, must give pause to those who take it for granted that Soviet cooperation will continue over the next year or two.

The second category of risk is that created by leaving the initiative to Saddam.

To date, Saddam Hussein's efforts to disrupt the coalition against him have been largely ineffective and somewhat ham-handed. They will undoubtedly continue. Saddam has had some success in marshaling the forces of Islamic fundamentalism against the U.S. presence in the Gulf. He will undoubtedly attempt to exploit the Palestinian conflict with Israel and engage in terrorist actions throughout the region. He could also withdraw partially from Kuwait in an effort to split the coalition.

Problems of Changing Current Policy

The manner in which the Bush administration has constructed the time line of this crisis creates another class of difficulty for anyone looking for a way to allow the sanctions more time to work. The administration has brought the UN Security Council and the anti-Iraq coalition along on its time line aimed at bringing the crisis to a head in late January or February.

It developed this way. On November 8, President Bush announced that the United States would almost double its forces deployed in the Gulf. Moreover, there would be no rotation of the forces that were there. On November 29, the United States, with strong support from Saudi Arabia and Egypt, won UN Security Council approval of a resolution authorizing the use of force if Iraq does not withdraw from Kuwait by January 15. As Secretary Baker told the House Foreign Affairs Committee on December 6, the international community had decided that five months is long enough to wait for sanctions to work.

Thus, a decision to rely primarily on sanctions would involve a switch not only in current U.S. policy, but in the policy and expectations of the other nations involved in the anti-Iraq effort.

Such a course would raise serious questions. The first concerns U.S. credibility, both with Saddam and with our coalition partners in the region. Can a military threat, once withheld, be made credible again to Saddam? Will the Saudis and the Egyptians support the military option in the future?

The second question concerns the sustainment of our military buildup. Can we maintain it a viable military option over a prolonged period or recreate it after an interval in which the deployed forces are placed in a more defensive posture?

Credibility

If, after January 15, Iraq still refuses to leave Kuwait and the United States, despite having secured UN authorization, is unwilling to use force, the world's perception of U.S. resolve is likely to change. The executive director of the Washington Institute for Near East Policy, Martin Indyk, told the committee that under these circumstances Saudi King Fahd would have to recalculate:

> Would he be better off cutting a deal with Saddam before we reduce our forces and before we make our own deal; or would he be better off embracing the long-term sanctions policy and hope he can rely on a still considerable American presence to defend against all those Iraqi forces deployed just north of the Saudi oil fields.
> The Saudi calculus will depend on several other factors: the credibility of our reassurances that we are there to stay; the commitment of other Arab allies (Egypt and Syria); the reaction of the Arab world to the U.S. strategy shift; and the impact of unforeseen events (instability in Jordan, a flare up of the Israeli-Palestinian conflict).
> We cannot know how all these factors will affect Saudi calculations . . . . Put simply, the longer it takes for sanctions to work, the more exposed Fahd will be to destabilizing factors, the more nervous he will be about the course he has adopted, the more doubtful he will be about American resolve, and the more open he will be to the alternative policy of "cutting a deal." That is why the Saudis are urging us to get it over with quickly: they doubt our staying power and they certainty doubt their own.

Thus, the prospects for an "Arab solution" or deal brokered by a third party could increase dramatically, although it is unlikely to be one to the U.S. liking.

Sustaining the Military Buildup

On December 12, the committee asked General Edward C. Meyer, former Army chief of staff, Larry Korb, former assistant secretary of defense for manpower, reserve affairs, and logistics, and General Duane Cassidy, former commander in chief of the U.S. Transportation Command and air force deputy chief of staff for manpower and personnel whether the United States was creating a "use-it-or-lose-it" deployment in the Gulf.

Their conclusion was that the United States could sustain a force of over 400,000 troops in the Gulf, but it would be difficult, costly, and require several important policy actions. First, there would have to be a rotation policy. Ground forces in Saudi Arabia could not maintain their fighting edge for more than six months, if that. General Meyer believed this would require the president to use his emergency powers to declare a partial mobilization, which would enable him to call up a million reservists.

Dr. Korb believed that our deployments in the Gulf would need to be rationalized: air force tactical units should replace carrier wings, army units should replace marines in Saudi Arabia, and our rapid contingency forces should be withdrawn. A logistical infrastructure for the expanded force would have to be built. Serious examination should be given to the possibility of reducing the force level while waiting for sanctions to work and then building it back up again when the president wanted an offensive military capability.

The committee asked Secretary of Defense Dick Cheney and General Powell to address this issue during their appearance before the committee on December 14. Their judgment agreed with that of our outside witnesses, namely that the U.S. buildup could be sustained although at great expense and with some difficulty.

Impact of a Sanctions Solution on U.S. Interests

No course of action is likely to secure all our interests in the Persian Gulf today. The UN goals—Iraq's unconditional withdrawal from Kuwait and the restoration of the legitimate government—addressed our interest in ensuring that aggression does not pay. Achieving security and stability in the region requires neutralizing Iraq's military leverage, both its million-man army and its growing capability for mass destruction weapons. Containing Iraq may be necessary, but is probably not sufficient for regional stability. The region has always been plagued by political instability and that is unlikely to change, no matter what happens to Saddam Hussein.

If sanctions "work," what have we achieved? If they force Saddam to withdraw completely from Kuwait, our government and the UN will have reversed Saddam Hussein's aggression. U.S. standing in the region will be stronger, and the UN, as a collective security mechanism, would have been strengthened. The immediate threat to oil and the region will have passed.

Neutralizing Iraq's Military Leverage

A sanctions solution, however, will still need to deal with the regional threat posed by Saddam's army and his interest in weapons of mass destruction.

Our expert witnesses were divided on whether Saddam himself would survive Iraq's withdrawal from Kuwait. He has already renounced his battlefield gains from the Iran–Iraq War and will have been forced to relinquish Kuwait after suffering devastating economic losses from the sanctions. As Ambassador Akins observed, Saddam is "too expensive" for the Iraqis. It is also possible, however, that Saddam could emerge as a hero in the Arab street. He had faced down the world and survived to fight another day.

The requirements for a post-crisis regional structure will be demanding because Iraq would still possess its military capabilities. They must be designed to ensure the independence of Saudi Arabia and the small Gulf states (without necessarily committing us too closely to the particular governments in place today), and they must attempt to constrain Iraq's level of military technology and its programs for missiles and weapons of mass destruction.

Some sort of peacekeeping force, perhaps under the UN flag or the Arab League, will have to be deployed to Kuwait. For the longer run, it is clearly desirable to avoid a large U.S. troop presence on the soil of Saudi Arabia. The Gulf states on their own do not have the potential to balance even a reduced Iraqi military. A promising alternative is to bind Egypt more closely to the Gulf Cooperation Council, having it provide manpower on the ground. The major U.S. role might be to maintain logistics facilities and pre-positioned equipment in the region (perhaps afloat) for a rapid reinsertion of force if necessary.

Such a regional security arrangement would need to be supplemented by measures to constrain Iraq's ability to develop nuclear weapons and ballistic missile technology. The evidence presented to the committee suggests that Iraq is not very far along on its quest to gain a uranium enrichment capability and that without major outside help it will take Iraq over a decade to achieve an operating enrichment capacity. This is clearly a subject that bears watching, as are Iraq's biological and chemical programs and its efforts in the missile area.

At the present time Iraqi missiles are not accurate enough to be militarily useful, although they can be used as terror weapons, particularly if armed with chemical or biological warfare agents. Its chemical warfare programs operate from day to day without outside assistance, but whether they can do so over the long term is unclear. Biological agents, though difficult to use militarily, are nearly impossible to constrain because of the kinship of their production processes with standard medical research techniques. Outside of immediate conflict, the one nuclear device Iraq might or might not be able to make on rapid notice with the IAEA safeguarded uranium seems less of a threat. The short-term nuclear threat could be dealt with easily through an enhanced inspection regime.

Finally, for the long run, the current crisis has made clear yet again that true peace on the Arab–Israel front would make other Middle Eastern problems more tractable. It is in Israel's paramount interest that progress toward such a peace be in train. No doubt it will take a while for a peace process to be rebuilt, but this should continue to be an objective of U.S. policy.

Conclusions

In this paper, I have attempted to assess the factors determining how the sanctions option works: what can they achieve, how might they be made to work, whether they can be sustained long enough to work and at what cost, and what are the implications of a solution arrived at by sanctions.

My review of the testimony presented to the committee has led me to draw several conclusions.

First, sanctions are working technically—superbly as a matter of fact. Iraqi oil exports have been shut down, its foreign exchange holdings are almost exhausted, and only a trickle of goods is coming in.

Second, technical success does not mean that sanctions will work politically by persuading Iraq to withdraw from Kuwait. Pain to the Iraqi people is not the same thing as pain to Saddam Hussein.

Third, those experts who believe that sanctions will work politically over time nevertheless conclude that it will take one to two years. Over that time, the pressure from sanctions must be reinforced by corresponding political, psychological, and military threats.

Fourth, I believe our coalition is too vulnerable, both economically and politically, to remain cohesive over the time it will take sanctions to work. Keeping up the requisite political, military, and psychological pressure to make sanctions works is the stumbling block. Can we keep the alliance together and focused long enough for sanctions to work politically? I judge the probability of that to be very low.

Fifth, I am very concerned about our loss of credibility in the region if the administration is forced to switch policy. The administration has brought the coalition along on a time line that will bring the crisis to a head on January 15. Walking the administration back from this policy could spell failure in this crisis. It could send a very dangerous message to Saddam Hussein and, if fact, make war more, not less, likely.

Finally, if we rely on sanctions to resolve the crisis, it will not deal with all of the concerns that we have in the region. Saddam's military machine remains intact and so does the threat to oil. Supplementary measures will be needed.

This report addresses the option of sanctions. I will soon be issuing my examination of two principal avenues for resolving the crisis—diplomacy and war. It is only through systematically examining all three options that we can make our final judgments on what we should do in the Persian Gulf.

3

Securing U.S. Interests in the Persian Gulf Through Diplomacy

December 28, 1990

Introduction

Hearings and Purpose of Report

On December 4, 1990, the House Armed Services Committee began a series of hearings on the Persian Gulf crisis. The purpose was to provide a systematic, thorough examination of the three main avenues for resolution of the conflict: sanctions, war, and diplomacy. The committee examined the costs and risks of each, what chance each option had of succeeding, and what success might mean in each case.

The committee dealt with sanctions during the first week of hearings and the military option during the second. I issued a White Paper with my views and analysis on sanctions on December 21, 1990, and plan to publish a paper on the military option in early January.

The third week of hearings examined the diplomatic option. The witnesses addressed all aspects of the issue: George Ball, former under secretary of state and ambassador to the United Nations, is a principal advocate of a diplomatic solution. Edward Heath, member of the British Parliament and former prime minister, has recently been to Baghdad where he obtained the release of some hostages and discussed diplomatic solutions. Joseph Sisco, former under secretary of state and a Middle Eastern specialist, and Helmut Sonnenfeldt, former counselor to the State Department and a visiting scholar at the Brookings Institution, assessed the impact of a diplomatic solution on U.S. interests in the region. Jeanne Kirkpatrick, former ambassador to the United Nations, and Cyrus Vance, former secretary of state, addressed the impact of diplomatic solutions on U.S. interests and the future world order.

This White Paper summarizes what I have drawn from these hearings and other sources on the diplomatic option. It is my report and not that of the House Committee on Armed Services. I offer it in hope of contributing to the substantive debate raised by the Persian Gulf crisis.

34

My analysis of the diplomatic option will address several key questions: how a diplomatic solution might be achieved, what it would accomplish, and its costs and long-term consequences. It is intended to help provide Congress the information it needs to carry out its constitutional responsibility.

U.S. Interests and Objectives

The invasion of Kuwait on August 2 confronted the U.S. government with three concerns. In three words, they were oil, aggression, and nukes.

The crisis in the Persian Gulf threatens fundamental and long-standing interests of the United States, regional stability in the Middle East. Iraq invaded and occupied Kuwait just as the cold war was ending. The rules that will govern the new world order are being fashioned in the crucible of this crisis. Saddam Hussein should not be allowed to enjoy the fruits of his aggression if we are to create a new, peaceful international order for the post-cold war era.

Rewarding aggression usually encourages more aggression, both from Saddam and other would-be Saddams. Thus, it is in our interest that the principle that aggression does not pay be reinforced by the resolution of this crisis. Otherwise, we face greater problems in the future.

Every president since Franklin D. Roosevelt has committed the United States to the pursuit of security and stability in the Persian Gulf. In part, this reflects our economic interest. The need of the United States and the world for reliable access to oil requires, in the short run, that Saddam Hussein's seizure of Kuwait's oil and attempt to dominate Gulf oil politics be opposed. In the long run, it requires security and stability in the Gulf where over half of the world's known oil reserves are located. Our pursuit of stability in the Gulf also stems from our concern about the security of important long-term allies and our general interest in stability as a prerequisite for economic growth and democracy.

Saddam Hussein's aggressiveness against a smaller, weaker neighbor destabilized the region. His million-man army, biological and chemical weapons, and coming nuclear capability pose a long-term threat to the region. Iraq's military leverage in the region must be neutralized if security and stability are to be achieved in the Persian Gulf.

As a matter of national policy, the United States is committed to the defense of Saudi Arabia and the UN-approved goals of ousting Iraq from Kuwait, restoring the Kuwaiti government, and freeing foreign nationals. This set of objectives, even though it does not address all of the U.S. interests at stake, has evolved as the bottom line for President Bush and most members of Congress and is often used as the litmus test for evaluating policy alternatives. A principal criterion for evaluating our options in the Gulf must be whether it accomplishes the UN objectives—that is, Iraq's unconditional and complete withdrawal from Kuwait and the restoration of the Kuwaiti government now that the hostages have been released.

What is Meant by a "Diplomatic Solution?"

The phrase "diplomatic solution" is imprecise, in part because there is a diplomatic aspect to all of the options for achieving U.S. objectives in the Gulf. The successful application of sanctions, threat of military action, or military action itself—all will result in a diplomatic end-game. On the other hand, the idea of a "negotiated solution" is too restrictive, because, as I will discuss later, there are several paths to a diplomatic outcome that do not involve the United States in any negotiations.

Here the phrase "diplomatic solution" refers to a settlement that is arrived at diplomatically, not primarily through the application of sanctions or military pressure. In the current context, the phrase "diplomatic solution" also implies a settlement that is reached soon, before sanctions have had time to work or the anti-Iraq coalition has resorted to force to achieve its objectives.

The Diplomatic Record To Date

Many Arab states, particularly Jordan and Algeria, have actively pursued a diplomatic solution from the onset of the crisis. The Arab Summit meeting held in Cairo on August 10 (which Saddam did not attend) reportedly considered, but did not adopt, a solution whereby Iraq would withdraw from Kuwait in return for various concessions: cancellation of war debts owed by Iraq to Kuwait, Saudi Arabia, and other Gulf states; compensation for oil allegedly extracted by Kuwait from the Rumaila oil field that straddles the border; an increase in oil prices; and long-term lease (or outright cession) to Iraq of two Kuwaiti islands (Bubiyan and Warbah) near the Iraqi Gulf port of Umm Qasr. This proposed solution is probably the most heavily pro-Iraq variant of the "Kuwaiti Payback Solutions," but is not atypical of most so-called Arab solution proposals.

Saddam Hussein quickly responded with what Iraqi officials now refer to as the "August 12 declaration." He said that he would not withdraw his forces until a comprehensive solution addressing "all issues of occupation" in the Middle East are resolved, including Israeli withdrawal from all occupied territories, Syrian withdrawal from Lebanon, and removal of U.S. and Egyptian forces from Saudi Arabia. Not surprisingly, the United States "categorically reject[ed]" the Iraqi proposal and called for the "immediate, unconditional and complete withdrawal of all Iraqi forces from Kuwait."

On August 15, Saddam Hussein proposed a peace initiative to Iran that included withdrawing Iraqi troops from Iran, agreeing to Iraq's position on the disputed pre-war borders, and releasing all prisoners of war. Iran accepted the terms, effectively ending the Iran–Iraq War. Saddam's dramatic renunciation of Iraq's battlefield gains, however, failed to prevent Iran from joining the UN-imposed economic embargo. Also on August 15, Iraq defined thousands of Americans and other Westerners as "restrictees" who were used as Saddam's bargaining chips and human shields for key Iraqi economic and military targets. Iraq subsequently announced it would hold foreign nationals until all foreign forces left the Middle East and the threat of war was ended.

On August 21, Iraqi Foreign Minister Aziz announced his country's willingness to hold direct talks with the United States to negotiate a settlement to the crisis. President Bush dismissed negotiations conditioned on Iraq's continued violation of international law regarding Kuwait and emphasized that the U.S. Embassy in Baghdad could conduct any "discussions."

Jordan's King Hussein announced on August 22 that he would fly to Baghdad and other Arab capitals in an effort to find a diplomatic solution and prevent the crisis from escalating. UN Secretary General Javier Perez de Cuellar said on August 26 that he would meet with the Iraqi foreign minister in Jordan. After two days of talks, de Cuellar reported on September 2 that he was disappointed by the lack of flexibility in Iraq's position on Kuwait. He also noted as "interesting" a proposal made by Libyan leader Qadhafi that called for the withdrawal of Iraqi forces from Kuwait and U.S. forces from Saudi Arabia. A UN force would move into Kuwait and an Arab force would replace U.S. troops in Saudi Arabia. Iraq would be given Kuwait's Bubiyan and Warbah islands.

President Bush and President Gorbachev reiterated their united stand on the Persian Gulf crisis after their meeting in Helsinki. They

demanded the complete and unconditional withdrawal of Iraqi troops
from Kuwait and reaffirmed their support for the five UN resolutions
passed at the time. They also agreed that if current measures were not
successful, then additional measures would be considered under the
UN Charter. President Gorbachev, however, spoke of a link between
the Persian Gulf crisis and the other problems of the Middle East and
advocated an energetic movement to resolve the disputes in the
region.

In a speech to the United Nations General Assembly on September
24, French President François Mitterrand put forward a four-stage
peace plan for the Middle East. Mitterrand said that:

> If Iraq were to affirm its intention to withdraw its troops and free
> the hostages, everything would be possible. At a later stage, the
> international community could be called on to guarantee the with-
> drawal of Iraqi forces and the restoration of the sovereignty of
> Kuwait and the democratic will of the Kuwaiti people.
>
> The third stage would involve an international conference aimed
> at resolving the civil war in Lebanon and the Arab–Israeli conflict.
> During the fourth stage of his peace plan, Mitterrand said the
> Mideast countries would make "mutually agreed arms reductions
> . . . stretching from Iran to Morocco, from the Mediterranean to the
> Atlantic."

Mitterrand's speech sparked considerable controversy and some
backtracking by French officials. The impression that a promise by
Saddam to leave Kuwait might be sufficient to lift the embargo was
soon "clarified"—only his unconditional and complete withdrawal would
suffice. Mitterrand's implication that some compromise on the nature of
the restored Kuwaiti government might be possible contrasted sharply
with Secretary Baker's comment the previous day that U.S. agreement
to a government in Kuwait without the Sabah family would be "ap-
peasement" of the kind that occurred in Europe in the 1930s. Baker
added that he "wouldn't want to see the world go down that road."
Paris subsequently reaffirmed its commitment to the restoration of the
legitimate government, but France, as well as most European Community countries, maintain that a resolution of the Gulf crisis should be
followed by an international conference on the Arab– Israeli conflict.

President Bush also spoke to the United Nations General Assembly
on October 1. He expressed hope that the crisis would be settled
peacefully, albeit on the terms set by the United Nations, but added
that opportunities would arise to settle regional problems such as that

between the Arabs and the Israelis following a complete withdrawal by Iraq from Kuwait. Although the president later said that he did not intend to link the Persian Gulf crisis with the Arab-Israeli conflict, most observers believed that he had made a tacit commitment, perhaps more to the Arab members of the anti-Iraq coalition than to Iraq, to address the Palestinian problem after the Gulf crisis was settled.

On October 3, French President Mitterrand began his visit to Saudi Arabia and the United Arab Emirates. President Gorbachev also sent, as his personal envoy to the Gulf, Yevgeniy Primakov, a Middle Eastern expert who reportedly believed that Soviet Foreign Minister Shevardnadze had tilted too much toward the U.S. position on the Gulf. Primakov spent three days in Jordan and Iraq, meeting with Saddam Hussein, King Hussein, and PLO Chairman Arafat, toured the Middle East and Europe, visited Washington, and returned to Baghdad later in the month. He then joined President Gorbachev in Madrid who, on October 29, advocated an Arab initiative aimed at achieving a diplomatic solution to the conflict. Gorbachev also said that a military solution was "unacceptable."

Algerian President Chadli Bendjedid met with Iraq's Deputy Prime Minister Taha Yasin Ramadan on October 15 and announced his opposition to any form of aggression against Iraq. He also endorsed Saddam's proposal for an international forum to resolve all Middle Eastern problems.

Saudi Arabia's defense minister, Prince Sultan, said on October 22 that his country would not oppose a Kuwaiti concession of territory as a "brotherly" gesture after Iraq had withdrawn from Kuwait. The next day, Saudi leader King Fahd and Saudi Ambassador to the U.S. Bandar clarified Prince Sultan's remarks, saying that the defense minister was not advocating any concessions in return for Iraq's withdrawal from Kuwait.

On November 11, Morocco's King Hassan proposed an emergency Arab summit meeting to discuss the Gulf crisis and avert a war in the region. Saudi Foreign Minister Saud al-Faysal said on November 14 that an Arab summit would be unfruitful. Egyptian President Hosni Mubarak and Syrian President Hafiz al-Asad said the following day that Iraqi preconditions had made such a summit difficult if not impossible.

On November 15 in an interview with ABC News, Saddam Hussein said he was willing to negotiate with Saudi Arabia and the United States toward a solution of the crisis. He would not, however, agree to the precondition of Iraqi withdrawal from Kuwait prior to negotiations.

The foreign ministers of China and the Soviet Union issued a joint statement urging a diplomatic solution to the crisis and praising the initiatives of Arab countries toward that end. The statement, which reiterated the demand that Iraq withdraw from Kuwait unconditionally and immediately, did not rule out the eventual use of force. On November 29, the Soviet Union voted for, and China abstained from, the UN Security council resolution authorizing the use of "all necessary means" if Iraq did not withdraw from Kuwait by January 15.

In efforts to "go the extra mile for peace," on November 30 President Bush invited Iraqi Foreign Minister Aziz to Washington and said he would send Secretary Baker to Baghdad to look Saddam Hussein "in the eye" and convince him that the United States was serious about using the authority granted by the UN on the previous day. Although administration officials insisted repeatedly that there would be no negotiating on the UN objectives, there were several "concessions" on other issues:

- In his November 30 initiative, President Bush echoed the theme struck in his October 1 speech to the UN by stating that "within the mandate of the United Nations resolutions, I will be prepared, and so will Secretary Baker, to discuss all aspects of the Gulf crisis."
- Although President Bush said he would invite ambassadors of several members of the anti-Iraq coalition to attend his meeting with Aziz, this was quietly dropped when Iraqi officials indicated that Saddam would invite his friends, including PLO leader Arafat, to attend his meeting with Baker.
- In a "Meet the Press" interview on December 2, Secretary Baker was asked if the United States would give assurances that it would not attack Iraq (in an effort to remove Saddam from power) if it withdrew from Kuwait. He responded that "we have never talked about force for anything beyond the UN resolutions."
- A week later, again on a Sunday talk show, Secretary Baker said the United States has "no problem" with talks between Kuwait and Iraq over their differences after Iraq withdraws completely from Kuwait. He added that, of course, the Kuwaiti's could count on firm U.S. backing so that the playing field would be level.

The sense of quickening movement on the diplomatic front grew when Saddam Hussein announced on December 7 that all Western hostages would be promptly released, thus fulfilling one of the central demands made on Iraq by the United States and the UN. The United States said that it would withdraw its diplomats from Kuwait as soon as the Iraqis made good on this promise, thus removing a possible provocation for war.

Nevertheless, there were still mixed signals from Baghdad. In its acceptance of the Bush initiative, the ruling Revolutionary Command Council used harsh language—President Bush was referred to as "the enemy of God"—and reiterated its adherence to Saddam's August 12 declaration, which ties any pullout from Kuwait to Syria's withdrawal from Lebanon and Israel's from the occupied territories. On December 10, Information Minister Latif Jasim dismissed speculation that release of the foreigners could be followed by Iraqi withdrawal from Kuwait as "dreams and wishful thinking." He added that "Kuwait is Iraqi, whether in the past, present or future" and that "we will not compromise one iota on Kuwaiti territory." On the same day, Foreign Minister Aziz refrained from such absolute statements and said that while Iraq would not respond to any U.S. threats or "ultimatums," it would "respond positively when it finds that there is good will on the side of the Americans." He suggested that Iraq was looking for a commitment by the United States to address the core Arab–Israeli dispute in a new dialogue because it is an underlying cause for many of the long-standing tensions in the region.

President Bush's offer started a flurry of Arab diplomatic contacts. Jordan's King Hussein recruited Algerian President Bendjedid in an effort to open a Iraq–Saudi channel to parallel the Iraq–American one opened by President Bush. On December 5, The European Community foreign ministers asked Iraqi Foreign Minister Aziz to meet with the Italian foreign minister after Aziz visited Washington. President Bendjedid, after consulting with several Arab leaders, went to Baghdad on December 13, but the Saudis announced on December 14 that it would not receive the Algerian leader. A Saudi official said there were "three conditions for anyone who comes to discuss a peaceful settlement" —Iraq's withdrawal from Kuwait, restoration of its legitimate government, and the "withdrawal of Iraqi troops from the Iraq–Saudi border." The *Washington Post* reported that this last condition had not been stressed before by Saudi officials, although it had been mentioned.

Moreover, the United States and Iraq could not reach agreement on when Secretary Baker should go to Baghdad. The United States offered to send Baker between December 20 and January 3 while the Iraqis insisted Saddam Hussein was too busy to see him until January 12. The latter was unacceptable to the United States because it was too close to the UN deadline of January 15 and could open the way for the Iraqis to try to get the deadline postponed. President Bush told reporters on December 14 that the Iraqi talks were "on hold" until Baghdad agreed to receive Secretary Baker before January 3. He noted, somewhat ominously, that the UN deadline "was real."

On the following day, Iraq announced that Foreign Minister Aziz would not depart for Washington as planned and that "Iraq alone" would set the date for Baker's visit. At this time, no date for talks has been set and war talk is mounting. President Bush reportedly told a congressional group that he has "crossed the Rubicon" in his Gulf policy and that Saddam must understand that "if we get into an armed situation, he's going to get his ass kicked."

How Can We Arrive at a Diplomatic Solution?

As the diplomatic record to date suggests, there are many different ways in which a diplomatic solution could be reached. The principal variants are

- Imposed by Iraq. Iraq could unilaterally withdraw from most, but not all, of Kuwait and might achieve a "partial solution" when the United States is unable to maintain international and domestic support for preventing Saddam from enjoying any rewards from his aggression. This has sometimes been referred to as the "nightmare scenario."
- An "Arab solution." Iraq and key Arab members of the anti-Iraq coalition strike a deal, perhaps along the lines suggested by the Saudi Arabian defense minister, without U.S. knowledge.
- Brokered by a third party. A third party, perhaps the UN secretary general, the Soviet Union, or France, could reach an accommodation with Saddam Hussein that is announced in Baghdad and the United States is unwilling or unable to overturn it.
- A U.S.-Iraq deal. The United States and Iraq reach an understanding through direct talks that is accepted by Washington's coalition partners.

The path by which a diplomatic solution is achieved would have a considerable impact on the perception of who won and who lost in the Gulf crisis.

Imposed by Iraq

The "nightmare scenario" in which Iraq partially withdraws from Kuwait, in effect presenting a deal by fiat and asking the world to accept it, remains a strong possibility. This is clearly not a solution the

United States could accept. It would, however, end the risk of war—neither the United States or its Arab partners would be likely to attack if Iraq held onto Bubiyan and Warbah islands and the sliver of Kuwait that contained the Rumaila oil field. But the allies would also be unlikely to lift the economic embargo, particularly on the export of oil. Saddam Hussein would have avoided war but not gained much relief from international pressure or ended the crisis. A "partial solution" may look good to Saddam, but only if it is actually a "solution" that includes the end of the economic embargo.

Arab or Third-Party Solution

At the present time, the probability of an "Arab solution" or a deal brokered by a third party seems fairly small. The Saudi refusal to even receive Algerian President Bendjedid in mid-December suggests that the anti-Iraq coalition is holding firm on the UN objectives. This also appears to be the case with the "third parties" that are the most likely candidates to broker a deal with Saddam Hussein, the UN, the Soviet Union, and France.

This could change, however, especially after the UN ultimatum of January 15 expires. If Iraq still refuses to leave Kuwait, and the United States, despite having secured UN authorization, is unwilling to use force, the world's perception of U.S. resolve could change. The executive director of the Washington Institute for Near East Policy, Martin Indyk, told the committee that under these circumstances Saudi King Fahd would have to recalculate

> Would he be better off cutting a deal with Saddam before we reduce our forces and before we make our own deal; or would he be better off embracing the long-term sanctions policy and hope he can rely on a still considerable U.S. presence to defend against all those Iraqi forces deployed just north of the Saudi oil fields.
>
> The Saudi calculus will depend on several other factors: the credibility of our reassurances that we are there to stay; the commitment of other Arab allies (Egypt and Syria); the reaction of the Arab world to the U.S. strategy shift; and the impact of unforeseen events (instability in Jordan, a flare up of the Israeli–Palestinian conflict).
>
> We cannot know how all these factors will affect Saudi calculations. . . . Put simply, the longer it takes for sanctions to work, the more exposed Fahd will be to destabilizing factors, the more

nervous he will be about the course he has adopted, the more doubtful he will be about American resolve and the more open he will be to the alternative policy of "cutting a deal." That is why the Saudis are urging us to get it over with quickly: they doubt our staying power and they certainty doubt their own.

Thus, the prospects for an "Arab solution" or a deal brokered by a third party could increase dramatically over time. It is unlikely to be one to the United States liking.

Direct Talks

A settlement arrived at through direct talks between the United States and Iraq may still be possible, even though the Baker–Aziz visits have yet to be scheduled. Bush administration officials have been adamant that there will be no "negotiating down" from the UN resolutions and that the sole purpose of Baker's trip to Baghdad is to convey the seriousness of U.S. purpose. The United States has given some informal assurances that the Iraqis might be receptive to no attack if Iraq withdraws completely from Kuwait and no objection to post-crisis talks between Kuwait and Iraq.

Is Saddam Hussein likely to agree to these? Some Middle Eastern experts believe so because they believe that Saddam has already decided, because of the threat posed by the U.S. buildup and the UN's authorization of the use of force, to withdraw from Kuwait. For example, Judith Kipper, a visiting scholar at the Brookings Institution, told the committee that "Direct talks with American officials may be the face-saving device that Saddam Hussein needs to withdraw from Kuwait."

Other analysts, including CIA Director Webster, believe that Saddam is not yet convinced that he must withdraw from Kuwait and instead will sit tight and try to stretch out the Gulf crisis until international resolve crumbles. Judge Webster told the *Washington Post* on December 14 that Saddam will not withdraw from Kuwait until convinced he "is in peril of imminent military attack" and that there is a danger that the Iraqi leader will continue to believe he can succeed "until the first shell is lobbed over him." If this characterization of Saddam Hussein is correct, the prospects of any diplomatic solution, much less one that could emerge from direct talks between the United States and Iraq, seem poor.

What is an Acceptable Diplomatic Solution?

UN Goals are the Litmus Test

The United States and other members of the anti-Iraq coalition have insisted that they would not accept anything less than the full compliance with UN resolutions. This is usually interpreted as meaning Iraq's complete and unconditional withdrawal from Kuwait and the restoration of the legitimate government. All of the witnesses appearing before the committee supported these goals with the exception of former British Prime Minister Edward Heath. He wanted talks between Iraq and the Kuwaiti-government-in-exile to begin "immediately," as called for in the first UN resolution passed on August 2, with the results presumably implemented in conjunction with an Iraqi withdrawal from Kuwait.

There is, however, the question of one UN goal, Iraqi reparations for its occupation of Kuwait. UN Security Resolution 674, which was adopted on October 29, declared Iraq responsible for all damage and personal injuries resulting from its occupation of Kuwait and asks nations to prepare claims for financial compensation and submit evidence of human rights violations by Iraqi forces. In effect, the United Nations laid the groundwork for reparations claims against Iraq, perhaps by seizing impounded Iraqi assets.

Most witnesses did not include payment of reparations in the same category as the other UN objectives. George Ball, for example, would leave the issue of reparations to talks between Iraq and Kuwait that would occur after Iraq's withdrawal. Jeanne Kirkpatrick, on the other hand, believed that "at a very minimum we must have compensation" from Iraq:

> After having destroyed Kuwait, thrown the region into upheaval, and cost the United States more than $30 billion and the other coalition members some $30 billion more, he should not escape without penalty. A settlement that fails to penalize him surely will not deter a future armed aggression. . . . If he escapes without penalty, he will be incalculably more dangerous to his neighbors.

Former Secretary of State Cyrus Vance also thought that reparations, both for compensation and punitive purposes, should be included in any settlement.

UN goals do not satisfy all U.S. interests

Some witnesses argued that immediate U.S. policy aims should extend beyond the UN objectives. Ms. Kirkpatrick, for example, believes that we should not accept any outcome that does not neutralize Saddam's military leverage:

> If he is allowed to keep this huge arsenal and to pursue his dream of a nuclear capability, he will soon be in a position to destabilize moderate Arab regimes, establish hegemony in the Gulf, control the flow of oil and its price, and emerge as a world power.

Virtually all of the witnesses appearing before the committee shared her concern, but most were willing to rely on post-crisis arrangements and mechanisms to deal with the future Iraqi threat. She, most emphatically, was not:

> It is grim to recall that the world sought no punishment—diplomatic, financial or other—for these violations [by Iraq] of the . . . Geneva Convention [prohibiting the initiation of chemical warfare]. Those who think we should now or in the future negotiate security arrangements with the Iraqi regime—regarding, for example, controls on Iraq's nuclear, chemical and biological weapons programs—should contemplate this sorry record. Iraqi cynicism about its legal obligations was matched by the self-interest and timidity of others.

Her belief that we should deprive Iraq of its military capacity to launch future aggressions, as well as her unwillingness to leave the task to the future, persuades her that "that there may be no alternative" to force for solving the crisis in the Persian Gulf.

Former Under Secretary of State Joseph Sisco shared Ms. Kirkpatrick's conviction that UN goals by themselves were not enough:

> It would have to be accompanied by measures to contain Saddam. Some of the elements of containment are a continued, but reduced, presence for an indefinite period of the U.S. and allied forces in Saudi Arabia; a UN presence in Kuwait; an ongoing naval flotilla in the Gulf and over the horizon; an agreement between the main suppliers to deny arms and technology to Iraq and insistence on tight inspection; the maintenance of sanctions at least until an agreement is reached to reduce and control arms; strengthening the

security relationship with Turkey, Egypt, and Saudi Arabia; a concerned effort by our European allies in particular to encourage Iran to become less ideological, more pragmatic, and to move toward closer mutual ties with the West, including the U.S.; and a reassessment of European policy which will define and undertake a more substantial sharing of burdens and responsibilities in the Gulf region for the long haul.

Mr. Sisco, however, was unwilling to use force to reduce this list of post-crisis tasks, arguing that we should resort to force only for the UN objectives.

Diplomatic options for achieving the UN goals

There are three principal types, each with many variants, of diplomatic solutions that could be packaged with the UN objectives:
- *Kuwaiti Payback.* Iraq withdraws from Kuwait with the understanding that territorial, financial, and/or political concessions from Kuwait will follow.
- *Treatment of Iraq.* Iraq withdraws from Kuwait in return for assurances on the post-crisis treatment of Iraq. The list of assurances could include items such as no attack from the anti-Iraq coalition, lifting of the economic embargo, lifting of the arms embargo, and no reparations for the occupation of Kuwait.
- *Linkage.* Iraq withdraws from Kuwait in return for actions on other issues that are "linked" to its compliance with the UN resolutions: the holding of an international conference on regional issues such as the Arab-Israeli conflict or Syrian occupation of Lebanon, the withdrawal of Western forces from the Gulf, or pricing policy concessions from OPEC.

The impact and implications of any particular diplomatic solution, of course, depend on what it consists of and how it is achieved.

The test of whether a particular diplomatic outcome is acceptable depends on its impact along two key dimensions:
- the impact on Iraq and prospects for regional security and stability;
- the impact on the United States, its standing in the region, and its role in the post-cold war era.

These are broad categories, but it is difficult to break them down further. We are interested in what happens to Iraq primarily because of the threat Iraq poses to security and stability in the Persian Gulf, a long-standing interest of the United States. The impact of a diplomatic solution on U.S. influence in the Persian Gulf would bear heavily on U.S. behavior in future situations.

Impact on Iraq and the Region

Almost any diplomatic solution, in all likelihood, will be trumpeted as a great victory by Saddam Hussein, and he has a good chance of having his views accepted by the Arab masses. Former Ambassador to Saudi Arabia Herman Eilts observed that U.S. credibility is "not high" because of the "widespread perception of the Arab masses (and of many, perhaps most Arab governments, including those in the anti-Iraq coalition), that the United States is irrevocably pro-Israeli and, as a corollary, anti-Arab, anti-Palestinian, and anti-Islamic."

Moreover, as Iraqi specialist Dr. Phebe Marr of the National Defense University noted, Saddam has reversed himself on several occasions and successfully put his own "spin" on it. She argues that Saddam Hussein could even withdraw totally and unilaterally from Kuwait and then claim that "he had 'stood up to America,' that he had succeeded in putting the Arab-Israeli problem on the international agenda, and that he changed the face of the Middle East for a decade." Moreover, Saddam, his army, and his nuclear, biological, and chemical capabilities will emerge intact if the crisis is resolved peacefully. That in itself is likely to be viewed as a victory in the Arab streets.

Despite the near certainty that a diplomatic solution will look like a "Saddam win" in the region, the critical test for the United States is whether the anti-Iraq coalition, in the wake of a diplomatic solution, will be able to hold together to contain Saddam and reduce Iraq's military leverage in the region. This will depend on the nature of a diplomatic solution:

- Too many "Kuwaiti Paybacks," particularly if they are thinly-disguised "quid pro quos," would reward Saddam's aggression, thus strengthening him and weakening his opponents. This would probably signal an era of Saddam-dominated Gulf politics.
- An "Easy on Iraq" solution—one that lifts the economic and arms embargo and imposes no reparations—also strengthens Saddam Hussein and makes it harder to contain him in the region. The arms embargo, at a minimum, needs to be kept in place, but we should try to get some military concessions from Saddam in return for lifting the embargo on his oil exports.

- The Arab members of the anti-Iraq coalition probably would welcome a "linkage" solution that tied Iraq's withdrawal from Kuwait to an international conference on the Arab–Israeli–Palestinian problem. Our relationship with Israel, however, would suffer greatly.

In short, our assessment of the impact of a particular diplomatic solution on the region should begin with the recognition that almost any outcome of the crisis that includes Saddam's survival is likely to be trumpeted as great victory for Saddam over President Bush, recently labeled in Iraqi propaganda as "the enemy of God." The extent to which it is actually a victory for Saddam Hussein depends on what the diplomatic solution consists of and how it is arrived at: How heavy are the Kuwaiti paybacks to Iraq? How easy is Iraq's post-crisis treatment? Is the anti-Iraq coalition intact? Is it strong enough to contain Saddam Hussein and neutralize Iraq's military leverage? And, finally, what concessions were made to Iraq on other issues?

Impact on U.S. and International Order

President Bush has committed the United States repeatedly and firmly to Iraq's unconditional compliance with the UN resolutions. A diplomatic solution that falls short of this would reward Iraqi aggression and damage U.S. credibility in that region and the world. From the U.S. perspective, it is almost a zero sum game—either Saddam Hussein wins or we win.

As Joseph Sisco observed, defining the line between "face-saving" concessions for Saddam and rewarding his aggression is difficult and "to some degree is in the eyes of the beholder." For example, he believed that a package that combined Iraq's withdrawal from Kuwait and the restoration of the legitimate government with a statement from us and our allies of our willingness to discuss outstanding Gulf issues (except the Palestinian issue) subsequent to Iraq's withdrawal would not constitute reward for aggression. Mr. Sisco, however, believed that George Ball's willingness to include the Palestinian issue would reward aggression and was therefore unacceptable.

In contrast to our Arab colleagues, we might be able to accept a deal that is heavier on the "Kuwaiti paybacks," provided their connection to the UN goals is well hidden. We would probably be just as concerned as they on how easy Iraq's post-crisis treatment is—the weaker Iraq is, the easier it is to contain. Because of our ties to Israel, we will take a much tougher stance on "linkage."

The United States successfully forged a UN consensus on goals and means (the use of force after January 15 if necessary) in the Gulf. A diplomatic solution that yields a clear Saddam "win" would reduce U.S. interest in relying on the UN in the future and would undercut the international order principle that aggression does not pay. Former Ambassador to Israel Samuel Lewis reported to the committee that a recent conference at the National Defense University concluded that the best outcome for the United States was a peaceful solution that achieved the U.S. objectives and that the worst outcome was a long, drawn-out war. The next worst outcome, the conference participants believed, was a diplomatic solution that gave Saddam a victory in the short term. It would be "disastrous" for U.S. interests in the region because our Arab allies would have to accommodate Saddam Hussein and would undermine the ability of the collective security mechanism in the United Nations to deal with the myriad of regional conflicts certain to emerge in the post–cold war era.

Conclusions

In this paper, I have attempted to assess the factors determining how the diplomacy option works: how might a diplomatic solution be achieved, what would it accomplish, and what are the costs and long-term consequences?

My review of the testimony presented to the committee has led me to draw several conclusions.

First, our ability to achieve an acceptable diplomatic solution depends on how much economic and military pressure we put on Saddam. The possibility of a diplomatic solution appears most promising now as we move toward the UN deadline of January 15. President Bush's offer to send Secretary Baker to Baghdad was the right move to make, and I hope Saddam Hussein decides to receive him.

Second, I believe the test of a diplomatic solution in the United States is the extent of compliance with the UN resolutions. The American people would regard a complete withdrawal by Saddam Hussein from Kuwait as victory almost regardless of what else is agreed upon around the edges.

Third, I believe the test of a diplomatic solution in the region is whether we can hold together the anti-Iraq coalition to contain Iraq in the future. No matter what the diplomatic result, Saddam will try to claim victory.

Fourth, as to some of the specifics we might offer to get a deal:

- We have already agreed that we will not attack Iraq if it withdraws from Kuwait and will not object to talks between the Iraqis and Kuwaitis after Iraq withdraws. I think this is correct policy.
- Although we might want to punish Saddam Hussein for his brutal plundering of Kuwait, I do not believe we should insist upon reparations as part of the deal. To date, the extraordinarily effective embargo against Iraqi oil exports has denied him the economic fruits of his aggression. As long as we achieve Iraq's complete and unconditional withdrawal from Iraq, we will have reversed that aggression and can claim victory over the aggressor.
- Iraq's partial withdrawal from Kuwait is not acceptable. It would, however, end the risk of war to Saddam—neither the United States or its Arab partners would be likely to attack if Iraq held onto Bubiyan and Warbah islands and the sliver of Kuwait that contained the Rumaila oil field. We would have to keep the sanctions in place to force his complete withdrawal.
- Although many of us understand that following this crisis the United States and its allies will turn to the Middle East peace process, we should not link it to Saddam's withdrawal from Kuwait. We cannot reward Saddam's aggression at the expense of our allies.

Finally, I believe that no outcome to the crisis will meet all of our concerns in the Gulf. Supplementary measures will be needed regardless of how the crisis is ended. For instance, at a minimum the arms embargo must be kept in place and we should attempt to negotiate military concessions from Saddam in return for lifting the embargo on his oil exports.

This report addresses the option of diplomacy. It follows my examination of the sanctions option that I issued on December 21, 1990. I will soon be issuing my examination of the war option. It is only through systematically examining all three options that we can make our final judgment on what we should do in the Persian Gulf.

4

The Military Option: The Conduct and Consequences of War in the Persian Gulf

January 8, 1991

Introduction

Hearings and Purpose of Report

On December 4, 1990, the House Armed Services Committee began a series of hearings on the Persian Gulf crisis. The purpose was to provide a systematic, thorough examination of the three main avenues for resolution of the conflict: sanctions, war, and diplomacy. The committee examined the costs and risks of each, what chance each option had of succeeding, and what success might mean in each case.

The committee dealt with sanctions during the first week of hearings, the military option during the second week, and the diplomatic avenue during the third. I issued a White Paper with my views and analysis on sanctions on December 21, 1990, and a second White Paper on the diplomatic option on December 28, 1990.

From December 12 through 17 the committee held five hearings on the military option. See Appendix B for hearing topics and witnesses.

This White Paper summarizes what I have drawn from these hearings and other sources on the military option. It is my report and not that of the House Committee on Armed Services. I offer it in hope of contributing to the substantive debate on the Persian Gulf crisis.

My analysis of the military option will address several key areas: the readiness of U.S. forces in the Persian Gulf, options for use of military force in the Gulf, the costs and risks associated with each option, the advantages and risks of relying upon force to resolve the Gulf crisis, and the implications for U.S. interests of a crisis solution arrived at through war. It is intended to help provide the information Congress needs to understand fully the costs and consequences of U.S. options and make an informed judgment as it carries out its constitutional responsibilities with regard to U.S. actions in the Persian Gulf.

U.S. Interests and Objectives in the Persian Gulf

The invasion of Kuwait on August 2, 1990, confronted the U.S. government with three concerns. In three words, they were oil, aggression, and nukes.

The crisis in the Persian Gulf threatens fundamental and long-standing interests of the United States and regional stability in the Middle East. Iraq invaded and occupied Kuwait just as the cold war was ending. The rules that will govern the world in the post-cold war era are being fashioned in the crucible of this crisis. Saddam Hussein should not be allowed to enjoy the fruits of his aggression if we are to create a new, peaceful international order.

Every president since Franklin D. Roosevelt has committed the United States to the pursuit of security and stability in the Persian Gulf. In part, this reflects our economic interest. The need of the United States and the world for reliable access to oil requires, in the short run, that Iraq's seizure of Kuwait's oil and attempt to dominate Gulf oil politics be opposed. In the long run, it requires security and stability in the Gulf where over half of the world's known oil reserves are located. Our pursuit of stability in the Gulf also stems from our concern about the security of long-term allies and our general interest in stability as a prerequisite for economic growth and democracy.

Under the leadership of Saddam Hussein, Iraq's aggressiveness against a smaller, weaker neighbor has destabilized the region. Iraq's million-man army, biological and chemical weapons, and coming nuclear capability pose a long-term threat to the region. Iraq's military leverage in the region must be neutralized if security and stability are to be achieved in the Persian Gulf.

As a matter of national policy, the United States is committed to the defense of Saudi Arabia and to the UN-approved goals of ousting Iraq from Kuwait, restoring the Kuwaiti government, and freeing foreign nationals. This set of objectives, even though it does not address all of the U.S. interests at stake, has evolved into the bottom line for President Bush and most members of Congress and is often used as the litmus test for evaluating policy alternatives. A principal criterion for evaluating an option in the Gulf must be whether it accomplishes the UN objectives—that is, Iraq's unconditional and complete withdrawal from Kuwait and the restoration of the Kuwaiti government now that the hostages have been released.

Strategic Objectives and Military Missions

U.S. Objectives in the Event of War

On November 29, 1990, the UN Security Council authorized the use of "all necessary means" to implement UN resolutions if Iraq does not comply with them by January 15. In the event that Saddam Hussein does not withdraw from Kuwait, the United States and its allies, whose military forces I will refer to as the "anti-Iraq coalition forces," will have UN authorization to use military force to make Iraq comply with the UN approved goals. Deciding whether to use force, however, requires a clear understanding of what our strategic objectives in a war with Iraq would be and what military missions are required to achieve them.

At a minimum, the anti-Iraq coalition forces will seek the following:
- The immediate, complete, and unconditional withdrawal of all Iraqi forces from Kuwait;
- The restoration of Kuwait's legitimate government.

A third principal objective—the release of foreign nationals in Iraq and Kuwait—was achieved on December 2, when Saddam Hussein announced that he would release all foreigners who wished to leave.

President Bush has stated repeatedly that the United States seeks security and stability in the Gulf, an objective that is shared by our allies. This latter goal has been interpreted variously to require:
- Reducing the war-making power of Iraq so that it is no longer a threat in the area;
- Eliminating Iraq's nuclear, biological, and chemical capabilities;
- Creating conditions that could lead to the fall of the Saddam Hussein regime;
- Establishing post-crisis regional security arrangements; and
- Establishing controls on arms sales and transfers of technology to Iraq.

The military option, of course, cannot by itself achieve all of these objectives. As would be the case with diplomacy or sanctions, supplementary measures will be needed. If, however, the United States and its allies decide to use force to obtain Iraq's complete withdrawal from Kuwait—the key test of an acceptable outcome to the crisis—they are likely to seek to accomplish two additional objectives:
- Reducing the size and effectiveness of Iraq's armed forces;
- Destroying as much of Iraq nuclear, biological, and chemical capability as possible.

Other objectives—such as driving Saddam from power—might be desirable, but are not likely to be adopted as wartime objectives by the anti-Iraq coalition.

Resulting Military Missions

These objectives translate into two broad missions for the anti-Iraq coalition forces:
- When ordered, undertake operations aimed at the liberation of Kuwait and the destruction of opposing Iraqi armed forces that occupy or threaten Kuwaiti territory;
- When ordered, conduct operations throughout Iraq and the Kuwaiti theater of operations to gain immediate air superiority and freedom of air action and destroy Iraqi nuclear, biological, chemical, and tactical ballistic missile capabilities.

These are well-defined and limited objectives. The anti-Iraq coalition does not appear to be seeking the conquest of Iraq or the punishment of the Iraqi people. In the event of war, strategic and military targets in Iraq are likely to be attacked, primarily by air power. Coalition air and ground forces would be used against Iraqi ground forces in Kuwait and the immediate area. There is little indication that non-military targets in Iraq will be targeted or ground forces used to seize Iraqi territory.

Coalition Forces

Strength and Dispositions in the Middle East as of January 1991

When planned and promised deployments are completed in January 1991, coalition forces in Saudi Arabia will total approximately 25 division equivalents, including almost 430,000 U.S. and 245,000 allied troops, equipped with 3,500 tanks and supported by over 1,300 naval and air force combat aircraft.

U.S. ground forces in the region include eight army division equivalents and supporting units and two marine expeditionary forces deployed ashore in Saudi Arabia and a marine expeditionary brigade and a marine expeditionary unit afloat in the Persian Gulf region. These forces are equipped with approximately 2,000 M1 and M1A1 tanks and are supported by over 1,000 combat and 250 transport aircraft.

Over 100,000 allied ground forces are deployed in the region. When the Saudi Arabian National Guard is included, the total increases to approximately 160,000. Two additional divisions promised by Egypt (4th Mechanized) and Syria (9th Mechanized) would increase the total by another 30,000–35,000. With increased force levels announced by the United Kingdom and by France, over 245,000 allied troops in addition to U.S. forces will be available.

Naval units afloat in the region in support of the force will include six carrier battle groups and two surface battle groups (battleships *Missouri* and *Wisconsin*), a total of approximately 90 surface combatants.

Readiness to Go to War

Events following the November 29 UN resolution have created the impression that the Bush administration was attempting to bring the Persian Gulf situation to a head by January 15. The readiness of U.S. forces to participate in offensive operations became an issue in late December. Would U.S. forces be capable of initiating combat operations soon after January 15 if Saddam Hussein did not withdraw from Iraq? If not, when would they be ready?

Getting the Force There and Insuring That It is Ready

On August 8, 1990, in response to the Iraqi invasion of Kuwait, the president ordered U.S. forces to the Persian Gulf with the mission to defend Saudi Arabia and deter further Iraqi aggression. The force totaled approximately 230,000 soldiers, sailors, marines, and airmen and included more than 660 U.S. combat aircraft and over 1,000 tanks. Deployed and proposed allied ground forces for the Middle East included up to 150,000 additional troops. The equivalent of 20 coalition force divisions—almost 400,000 troops equipped with 2,500 tanks and supported by over 900 naval and air force combat aircraft—were scheduled to be in the region by November 1. Completion of the deployment slipped to early December because of transportation delays.

In late October, press reports suggested that additional force requirements were being considered by the chairman of the Joint Chiefs of Staff, General Colin Powell, and the commander of U.S. forces in the Persian Gulf, General Norman Schwarzkopf. In addition,

Pentagon planners reportedly wanted to replace the 82nd Airborne Division with heavier forces and were designating additional units that might be sent to the Gulf as rotational units or reinforcements. General Powell reported to the committee on December 14 that in late October he had consulted with General Schwarzkopf and the Joint Chiefs of Staff on the force levels required to provide our forces in the Gulf with an offensive capability.

On November 8, President Bush announced that the U.S. forces in the Persian Gulf would be almost doubled in size so that a credible "offensive military option" would be available against Iraq. The additional deployment included an army corps of 3½ division equivalents, an additional marine expeditionary force, three carrier and one surface battle groups, and 14 additional fighter, two bomber, and 11 support aircraft squadrons—a total of approximately 150,000 troops, 650 additional air force, navy, and marine combat aircraft, and 1,100 additional M1A1 and M1 tanks. Subsequently, the United Kingdom announced that it would send a second armored brigade to Saudi Arabia, and France increased its deployments as well.

On November 29, 1990, the UN Security Council authorized the use of force if Iraq did not leave Kuwait by January 15, 1991.

On December 14, General Powell told the House Armed Services Committee that the additional deployment announced by the president "would take two or three months" from November 9 to complete the "Phase II" buildup of U.S. and anti-Iraq coalition forces offensive capability. In other words, General Powell seem to believe the buildup would be completed by early February, if not sooner.

During the week of December 18, Lt. General Waller, deputy commander to General Schwarzkopf, told the press in Saudi Arabia that "every unit will not be fully combat ready until after the first of February sometime." Press reports also indicated that the flow of equipment within and from Europe had been delayed by bad weather.

On December 26, the *Wall Street Journal* reported that according to Pentagon officials, Secretary of Defense Dick Cheney had advised the White House of General Schwarzkopf's assessment that ground forces would not be fully prepared for an all-out assault until February. General Schwarzkopf apparently believed that extra time was important to build up supplies of munitions and high technology missiles, improve coordination, and ensure proper training of recently arrived troops.

Units arriving in the Gulf earlier this year required several weeks to marry up with their equipment after arriving in Saudi Arabia to become used to the weather and prepare for desert operations. It apparently takes two to three weeks following arrival in the theater for troops to become prepared for combat, as indicated by comments from those in the theater and by military analysts in this country. Lt. Colonel Glynn Pope, U.S. Army, told CBS news on December 9 that "It takes two or three good weeks of hard, hard work out there." Retired Marine General George Crist noted that "Even after all our forces are there, its going to take up to a month to get fully combat-ready to fight in the desert and conduct an operation as complex as an offensive."

Will we be ready on January 15? Readiness is not an all-or-nothing proposition in individual units nor in the overall picture of U.S. forces in Saudi Arabia. It is not the case that units are not ready on Monday and then ready on Tuesday. It is always a matter of degree.

As our expert witnesses and others have indicated, units newly arrived in the Persian Gulf require some time to acclimate and bring themselves to peak readiness. Many of those forces already in country or on station have done so.

U.S. Air Force and U.S. Navy units will be fully available and ready on January 15. Those ground combat forces deployed after August 9 will likewise be ready. Those ground units deployed after November 8 will not have fully completed their preparation for combat operations. Our forces would certainly be capable of mounting some kind of offensive operation after January 15, but it appears that a couple more weeks could make a difference.

Coalition Force Strengths

U.S. and allied forces in the Persian Gulf should enjoy four principal advantages over Iraqi forces: air power, the ability to fight at night, superior strategic and tactical intelligence, and superior logistics.

First, the coalition's air power provides the clearest and most one-sided advantage enjoyed by the anti-Iraq forces. Coalition forces will have an almost three to one edge in numbers of combat aircraft and an overwhelming edge qualitatively. Given the uneven quality of the Iraqi Air Force and their inexperience in offensive counter air and air defense operations, coalition forces should be able to establish air superiority relatively easily over Kuwait and over Iraq, as well. Military analysts estimates for the time required to establish air superiority ranged from one to a few days. Control of the air in a part of the world where there is little to no concealment available for deployed forces will permit coalition air forces to range over both Iraq and the battlefield and attack strategic and tactical targets at will.

Second, the U.S. Army enjoys a marked edge in night fighting capability. Its night vision devices are widely distributed among individual soldiers, armored fighting vehicles, and attack and scout helicopters and give the army unparalleled night-fighting capabilities. Unfortunately, the Marine Corps and the majority of other coalition forces do not possess this capability to the same degree.

Third, the superior logistical support available to U.S. and other allied forces provides the anti-Iraq coalition with a clear advantage over Iraq, whose ability to sustain its forces is questionable under the combined effects of an embargo and an effective interdiction campaign. As General Meyer said to the committee on December 12, ". . . logistic support drives the tactics . . . ." The U.S. logistical system and the ability to maintain it free from any interference by Iraqi air and tactical ballistic missile attack (assuming that our air operations are as successful as is expected) will provide a marked advantage. The Saudis apparently will provide separate logistical support for Syrian, French, and Egyptian forces. It may not be as good as that provided to U.S. and British troops, but is still likely to exceed that provided by Iraq to its forces.

Finally, the coalition forces will have a marked advantage in both strategic and tactical intelligence as a result of the U.S. space-based capability and intelligence platforms that have been deployed into the region. When coupled with the strike capability present in U.S. conventional strategic and tactical air, the combined target acquisition and attack capability of the anti-Iraq coalition forces should dictate the course of the war.

Key Uncertainties

There are four principal questions with respect to the military capability of the coalition forces: In the event of war, who will join the fight against Iraq and where will they fight? Would an Iraqi attempt to involve Israel in the war lead to the breakup of the anti-Iraq coalition? Is the command and control of the coalition forces adequate? Can the coalition forces protect the Saudi oil fields?

First, the willingness of our key allies to fight is an enormously sensitive subject about which governments are reluctant to comment publicly. What is stated publicly, including perhaps comments several months ago by Egyptian and Syrian field commanders that their forces were present only for defensive purposes, is often aimed at domestic audiences and does not reflect actual intentions. Secretary of Defense

Cheney addressed this question very cautiously when he appeared before the committee on December 14:

> Each nation that has deployed forces to the region has worked out an arrangement if you will, those who have troops in Saudi Arabia with the Saudis. I am sure there probably are varying levels of commitment. Their commitment now is to have forces there. Some of them are fully committed to defending Saudi Arabia should there be conflict and some of them, I would guess, would go further and join in an effort to liberate Kuwait. So it varies. Each one of those governments will have to make in a sense a political decision as to whether or not they would participate in the kind of action that would be required were we to use force to implement the UN resolutions.

The former commander of the Allied Air Forces in Central Europe, General Charles Donnelly, USAF (Ret.), told the committee on December 13 that he believed that it was easier to determine who would participate in air operations than it was for ground operations. Based on his experience in the region, he believed that Arab, British, and French air forces would participate in any air campaign against Iraq as part of the effort to get them out of Kuwait.

The Economist addressed, on January 5, the issue of alliance participation in a Gulf war and reached an ambiguous conclusion. It reported that Egyptian officials close to President Mubarak indicated that Egyptian forces would fight Iraqi forces in Kuwait but not "penetrate Iraq itself." Western diplomats in Damascus reportedly believed that while Syria wouldn't block an attack on Iraq, it also wouldn't participate. *The Economist* noted, however, that Egyptian and Syrian forces come under direct Saudi command and the Saudis appear confident that they will obey whatever orders are given.

The willingness of our principal allies to join, if necessary, an attack against Iraq is critical, both politically and militarily. In the event of a war, U.S. air power would be used against strategic and military targets in Iraq and Kuwait and U.S. ground forces against the Iraqi Army deployed in or near Kuwait. Based on innumerable conversations I have had with U.S. and allied officials, I am confident that our forces will be accompanied by most, if not all, of our principal allies in both missions. In particular, I believe that Arab forces are willing to engage Iraqi forces in Kuwait. Attacks on Iraqi forces in Iraq are more problematic. We should plan accordingly.

Second, the probability seems very high that, if attacked, Iraq will attack Israel in an effort to break up the opposing coalition by widening an anti-Iraq war into an Arab–Israeli one. Iraqi officials, including Saddam Hussein (most recently in late December on Spanish television), have stated repeatedly that Tel Aviv would be the first Iraqi target in the event of war. Iraq also test-fired several surface-to-surface missiles in late December, reportedly not in the direction of the coalition forces in Saudi Arabia but, in all likelihood, in the direction of Israel. Israel responded with its own test-firing of a medium-range surface-to-surface missile.

Israeli concern over this threat peaked in late November when several Israeli defense officials implied that they might consider preemptive action against Iraqi missiles aimed at Israel, in part because of frustration over what they believed was inadequate intelligence-sharing and military coordination with the United States. A preemptive attack by the Israelis, of course, would be much more damaging to the cohesion of the anti-Iraq coalition than an Israeli response, particularly in kind, to an Iraqi first strike.

Israel clearly was reassured after Prime Minister Yitzhak Shamir's visit to Washington in mid-December when, according to the Israeli press, President Bush strongly reaffirmed the U.S. commitment to Israel's security if attacked and reached an agreement with Prime Minister Shamir on strategic cooperation if a war should break out. Israeli Defense Minister Moshe Arens subsequently said on Israeli radio that "we are not in the business of launching preemptive strikes" and told Parliament on December 25:

> We do not rule out the possibility of the Iraqis striking at us first. Saddam Hussein's missiles have the range to reach Israel. But their capability is very restricted. If we are hit, we shall strike back. But there is no need for panic.

Former Ambassador to Israel Samuel Lewis and former Assistant Secretary of State for the Middle East Richard Murphy both believed that there was "no question" that Israel would respond if attacked, but thought that our principal Arab partners, while disturbed by the impression that they were allied with Israel in a fight against a brother Arab, would continue to fight. A disproportionate or lengthy Israeli retaliation, of course, would create more public pressure, particularly on Syria and Egypt, to pull out of the fight against Iraq.

The impact of Israel's potential involvement upon the willingness of our Arab allies to fight Iraq is an exceptionally sensitive subject about which little can be said publicly by official sources. I have no doubt that the issue has been discussed extensively by all the parties concerned. My reading of recent Israeli statements is that they have agreed to stay out of the war unless attacked and, if attacked, will respond quickly and in kind, much like the one-shot retaliatory raids they have launched in the past after Palestinian terrorist attacks. I also believe that our Arab allies expect this and will continue fighting. What they would find difficult is Israel's entering the war on a sustained basis, which I do not think is likely. In short, although Saddam Hussein probably will try to split the forces arrayed against him by attacking Israel, I believe the attempt will fail.

Third, several military commentators have questioned whether the multinational forces opposing Iraq have adequate command and control. Ideally, it would be desirable to fully integrate the national commands into a unified joint command. This happened in Korea, but this has proven to be the exception, not the rule. Historically, nations have coordinated their military operations, with each assuming separate spheres of responsibility, rather than forming a unified command structure. Political, not military, considerations have usually been the cause.

The anti-Iraq coalition has established parallel commands for U.S. and Arab forces. U.S., British, and now (in the event of hostilities) French forces operate under U.S. command, while Arab forces operate under Saudi Arabian command:

- General Schwarzkopf, the U.S. Central Command commander, is the commander of all U.S. forces participating in Operation Desert Shield and also exercises control over attached British forces. His joint force is organized with army, air force, marine, naval, and special operations component commands.
- Saudi Arabian Defense Minister Prince Khalid commands all Arab and Islamic national forces, including those of Syria and Egypt.
- U.S. and Saudi commanders have established a co-located command center from which to direct operations.
- Air forces operate under a combined air operations center coordinated through the U.S. Air Force component command.
- The U.S. Naval component command coordinates naval operations in the Persian Gulf and assists with the coordination of the multinational interception force in the Gulf of Oman and the Red Sea.

Secretary Baker and Saudi King Fahd reached agreement in early November that the United States would have responsibility for planning all offensive operations outside of Saudi territory and operational control of all forces if offensive military action were taken.

In October, following a trip to the Middle East, General Powell reported that General Schwarzkopf had expressed his satisfaction with the command arrangements. In his prepared statement before the committee on December 14, General Powell stated:

> The multinational command and control is an evolving process but thus far has been very successful. Although a unified command structure is desired, coordination and cooperation (recognizing and accommodating national sensitivities) between the multinational forces have provided an effective force to deal with the changing situation. . . . Close coordination exists . . . . This arrangement is working well . . . .

It is my belief that General Powell's assessment is correct. Political realities rule out the creation of a fully integrated command structure for the anti-Iraq forces. It is also apparent that the coalition forces are making efforts to improve their ability to coordinate their activities in the event of a war. I am satisfied that command and control arrangements, while not ideal, are satisfactory.

Third, Saddam Hussein's threat to turn the entire region into a "sea of fire" raises the issue of whether the anti-Iraq coalition forces can protect the Saudi oil fields. On January 2, delegates to an international science conference in London on the possible impact of a Gulf war said that pollution from blazing oil installations and from oil spillage could threaten the world's ecology and even cause disastrous climate changes. Concern has also been expressed that Iraqi attacks on Saudi oil fields would damage them so much that world access to Saudi oil would be effectively denied.

The Iraqi options for attacking are few in number and limited:

- Iraq lost the ability to attack the oil fields from the ground when U.S. ground and air forces arrived in Saudi Arabia after August 9.
- Iraqi aircraft and tactical ballistic missiles undoubtedly would be targeted against the oil fields. They also would be high-priority targets in the initial stages of any coalition offensive action. Some aircraft and missiles will survive, but their ability to attack the Saudi oil fields with either conventional or unconventional weapons would be limited.
- Iraq was unable to interdict the Iranian oil flow during the Iran–Iraq War despite limited Iranian air defenses. It is not likely

- to be much more successful against the much more heavily defended Saudi facilities.
- Iraq's tactical ballistic missiles could cause some damage if key elements in a refinery or distribution center were successfully targeted. The Scud-B is a relatively inaccurate missile, however, and more suitable for delivery of a nuclear weapon against a large area target than of a relatively small conventional warhead against an oil well or refinery. Iraq's longer range missiles are less accurate and have even smaller warheads.
- Although there have been a few incidents of sabotage or terrorist attacks against Saudi oil facilities, an effective campaign against Saudi field installations would require an indigenous terrorist support network. Random terrorist attacks are a possibility that should not be discounted, but are not likely to have a major impact on overall Saudi oil production.

In the event of a war, the Kuwaiti oil fields, which, according to press reports, may have been mined and rigged for demolition by the Iraqis, will undoubtedly suffer additional damage. The market has already adjusted for the absence of Kuwaiti and Iraqi oil, however. Iraq's capability against the Saudi oil fields is limited and is not likely to have a significant effect on Saudi oil production.

To summarize, I have been concerned about all four of these uncertainties that could affect the capability of the coalition forces and have spent considerable time analyzing them. I am least worried about our ability to protect the Saudi oil fields and to have adequate command and control, but most concerned about the impact that an Iraqi attack on Israel might have on the cohesion of the anti-Iraq coalition. Nevertheless, it is my judgment that these problems are under control, but I list them as "uncertainties" because I am not 100 percent sure.

Iraqi Forces

Strength and Disposition

On August 2, 1990, Iraq invaded Kuwait, defeated the Iraqi armed forces, and established control over the country within 36 hours. Since that time Iraq has reinforced its forces in southern Iraq and in Kuwait. Estimates of Iraqi forces deployed in the Kuwaiti theater of operations total over 500,000 soldiers, organized in some 30-plus divisions with approximately 4,000 tanks, 2,500 armored personnel carriers and infantry fighting vehicles, and 2,700 artillery pieces, supported by up to 500 combat aircraft. Iraq continues to mobilize forces for possible employment against the coalition and has recently called up its class of 17-year-old males. Most military analysts, however, believe that Iraq is reaching the bottom of its manpower pool and will have great difficulty in significantly expanding its armed forces.

Iraq's first tactical echelon, composed primarily of infantry divisions, is established in prepared defensive positions in a series of man-made obstacles along the Kuwait–Saudi Arabian border. A tactical reserve force, predominantly armored and mechanized divisions, is deployed in central Kuwait. The Iraqi second operational echelon, including an estimated five elite Republican Guards divisions, is along and north of the Iraq–Kuwait border south of Basra. Two Republican Guards divisions are reportedly in the vicinity of Baghdad. Additional units are deployed along the Syrian, Turkish, and Iranian borders.

Iraqi Strengths and Weaknesses

The Iraqi armed forces include an army that has been tested in battle in the desert as a result of the long war with Iran. They have mass and a significant chemical capability that they have used before. Iraq's air force is weak. They have a logistical system that, although good by Third World standards, is vulnerable to interdiction. The Iraqi army has never experienced the effects of a serious air campaign.

Iraq's greatest strength is its ground forces. The Iraqi Regular Army and the Republican Guards represent a professionally competent, well-equipped, well-led, and well-trained force with considerable experience in combined arms warfare gained during the Iran–Iraq War. Their force of 5,000 tanks and 3,500 guns is equipped with a wide variety of Soviet, Western, and Third World equipment and includes some of the most modern equipment, as well as equipment of 1950s vintage.

Based on the record of the Iran–Iraq War, the Iraqi army appears to excel in the ability to conduct a position defense from well-prepared positions backed up by substantial mobile reserves. In Kuwait, Iraqi ground forces appear to be relying heavily on past experience as they establish strongly fortified defensive positions along the coast of Kuwait, the southern border with Saudi Arabia, and the western border of Kuwait, with a network of north–south and east–west military roads behind them to support the rapid movement of both supplies and tank and mechanized reserve forces.

The Iraqi army depends upon attack helicopters for close air support. Their field artillery, which is organized and trained along the Soviet model, was very effective in the latter stages of the Iran–Iraq War. They possess a large number of air defense weapons, but their capability to mount an integrated air defense is generally regarded as weak.

Second, the Iraqi chemical capability is extensive, including blister, blood, and nerve agents, and was repeatedly used in the Iran–Iraq War. The Iraqis apparently included chemical fires in their normal defensive fire plans and in some offensive fire plans as well. The favorite targets for Iraqi chemical weapons included artillery positions, assembly areas, and Iranian command and control facilities.

Third, Iraq's greatest weakness may lie in its poor air force and inferior air defense forces. During the Iran–Iraq War, the Iraq air force was largely ineffective, confining itself to inaccurate high altitude attacks against Iranian cities after initially taking losses from limited Iranian air defense. The Iraqi air force can be expected to be even less effective against much more extensive and sophisticated U.S. and Saudi air defenses. Iraqi pilots have also shown a marked reluctance to engage in air defense and counter-air operations.

Iraq possesses a large number of air defense weapons, but their capability to mount an integrated air defense is generally regarded as weak. Former Strategic Air Commander General Russell Dougherty and General Donnelly both told the committee that it should be relatively easy with modern weapons to defeat the Iraqi air defense system. The Iraqi army would still retain, however, a relatively large number of air defense guns and hand-held missile systems that would pose a threat to low-flying aircraft.

Fourth, while the Iraqi logistics systems is impressive for a Third World military, it is very vulnerable to air attacks. During the Iran–Iraq War, the Iraqis fought and were supplied along a 750-mile front by a stable and fixed supply line and logistics infrastructure. Material was shipped from one transhipment point to another as supplies were moved forward almost in "fire-bucket brigade" fashion. This worked well against Iran, which had limited-to-no ability to interdict.

In Kuwait, major supply depots have been withdrawn and are established in southern Iraq. Although a network of military roads has been established to facilitate the movement of supplies and reserves, these would be very vulnerable to air interdiction in a area that has little cover or concealment and excellent visibility.

Key Uncertainties

From the perspective of the anti-Iraq coalition, there are two principal questions concerning Iraqi military capabilities: How well will the Iraqi soldier stand up to a sustained air campaign? How effective will Iraq's chemical and biological weapons be?

First, many Egyptian and Saudi officials privately disparage the Iraqi soldier's will to fight. Egyptian President Mubarak reportedly told a visiting committee delegation that he has a very low regard for the capabilities of the Iraqi military based on their performance in the 1973 Arab–Israeli War. Comments by several recently returned Westerners from Kuwait suggested that Iraqi soldiers appeared more battle-weary than battle-tested. Others pointed to the lack of discipline displayed by many Iraqi soldiers during the invasion and looting of Kuwait.

On the other hand, Stephen Pelletiere and Douglas Johnson, authors of a recent Army War College study of Iraq's performance during the Iran–Iraq War, view the Iraqi army as a competent, reasonably well-equipped, and well-trained force with considerable experience in desert warfare and combined arms operations gained during the Iran–Iraq War.

Clearly, the elite Republican Guard units are highly motivated and capable forces, as are the armored and mechanized groups of the Regular Army. The militia-like Popular Army forces are probably the least motivated and capable forces. The Regular Army's infantry divisions, which provide the bulk of Iraq's first echelon forces, fall somewhere in between. General Powell told the committee on December 14 that

> The Iraqi army has strengths . . . some very, very competent units, that are well led, commanders with operational experience. . . . We take those units very, very seriously . . . . [There are] other units that are clearly less capable. We understand their weaknesses and vulnerabilities . . . . I certainly hope President Mubarak ['s assessment of the quality of Iraqi forces] is right. But . . . we don't have to take a chance on underestimating the enemy.

The Iraqi army, however, has never come under sustained, heavy air attacks. General Dougherty told the committee that in the 1973 Arab–Israeli war, Egyptian soldiers performed well when they were protected from the threat of Israeli air, but their fighting qualities were severely degraded when under heavy air attack. The noted military analyst and historian Colonel Trevor Dupuy, USA (Ret.), added that in the 1967 Arab–Israeli war, Israeli air power had a devastating impact on Arab troops who certainly "were not cowards," but nevertheless were panicked when "attacked by unhampered, unhindered air power." The former commander of the U.S. Army Training and Doctrine Command, General William DePuy, USA (Ret.), maintained that

> it all depends on how effective the U.S. forces are in attacking them. . . . If the attack is inefficient and ineffective and unsuccessful, they [the Iraqis] will be there tomorrow morning. If the attacks are in general effective, quick, devastating and lethal, the word will get around, and the second and third-class troops will begin to fade away.

Second, while there is little doubt that Iraq will use chemical and, perhaps, biological weapons during the course of a war, there is considerable dispute over how effective these weapons would be. Iraq employed chemical weapons repeatedly in the Iran–Iraq War, and Saddam also employed chemical weapons domestically against the Kurds. They have a substantial stockpile of chemical weapons deliverable by artillery, aircraft, and missile and probably have some biological weapons as well.

In a hot desert environment, chemical agents dissipate fairly quickly and are relatively limited in their casualty effect. Nevertheless, the presence of a chemical threat is psychologically debilitating to opposing troops and the requirement to wear chemical protective equipment can sharply reduce the effectiveness of ground troops due to excessive heat.

Nevertheless, a noted specialist on chemical weapons, Brad Roberts of the Center for Strategic and International Studies, told the committee on December 6 that he did not view the Iraqi chemical and biological capabilities as very significant militarily. While acknowledging that Iraqi chemical-equipped missiles could constitute an effective "terror weapon" against urban targets, Iraq's short range capability is probably not large enough to sustain continuous or large scale chemical operations.

Principal Scenarios and Options for War in the Persian Gulf

During the course of the committee's hearings on the military option, plausible military scenarios for alternative offensive military operations in the Persian Gulf were presented by military analysts as a basis for discussion by panels of retired senior military officers. The purpose was not to attempt to second-guess active operational planning, but to permit members of the committee to gain an understanding of the ability of various alternatives to achieve U.S. and UN objectives and of the conduct, likely costs, and uncertainties of each alternative.

The public debate over how a war might be fought in the Persian Gulf, as well as testimony before the committee, indicates that there are two schools of thought on how a military offensive against Iraq should be conducted—one that calls for total reliance on air power and another that insists that ground forces will be required.

Air power advocates believe that air power alone can achieve the UN objectives, either by forcing the Iraqi leadership to withdraw their forces from Kuwait or destroying Iraqi forces from the air. For example, the director of strategic studies at the Paul A. Nitze School of Advanced International Studies at Johns Hopkins University, Eliot Cohen, told the committee that an air campaign largely targeted against Iraq would result in the "visible destruction of much of the Iraqi armed forces and economy, the enfeeblement of the Baathist system of political control, the demonstration of complete vulnerability to American power, and the crumbling of a besieged and suffering garrison in Kuwait" that would "either lead Saddam to yield, or lead others to depose him and deal with us." Edward Luttwak of the Center for Strategic and International Studies is also convinced that an air campaign against Iraq would convince Saddam and the Iraqi leadership to withdraw their forces from Kuwait rather than risk continued destruction of those strategic and infrastructure targets they regard as critical.

Hans G. Stoll, U.S. Air Force fellow at the Center for Strategic and International Studies, argued in the *Miami Herald* on December 17 that

> An independent air campaign, if properly applied, would ensure the quickest and least costly route to victory. Air power's inherent characteristics of speed, range, flexibility, precision, and lethality create an attractive means of forcing Iraq to withdraw permanently from Kuwait and "neutralize" Hussein's capability to wage war for the foreseeable future. . . . Air is a no-lose proposition. Even if air power cannot secure victory within a "reasonable" period given to it, then its combat power can be brought to bear directly against Iraqi ground forces in Kuwait. The enemy will have been sufficiently weakened by this time to allow Arab ground forces to reoccupy Kuwait with few U.S. casualties.

Colonel Dupuy's statement to the committee acknowledged that the proponents of air power might be right in this instance:

> Air operations alone against politico-military and military targets just might work. Historically, no previous effort to defeat ground opponents by air power alone has succeed unequivocally, and most such efforts have failed. But the circumstances now existing are very different from those examples of failure. Contributing to air capability under these circumstances are the greatly improved ability of very lethal air-delivered weapons to hit and destroy ground targets, and [the] availability of a formidable ground force for immediate employment to overwhelm survivors, if necessary, and to occupy the ground, since air power cannot occupy ground areas.

Opponents of the air power advocates, however, argue air power alone has never won a war in the past and would not win one in the Persian Gulf. It was the view of most of the retired senior military officers and military analysts who appeared before the committee that our military plans for the Persian Gulf must be based on the assumption that a combined or integrated air-ground campaign would be necessary to defeat the Iraqi army and liberate Kuwait. To some extent, this reflected tradition: General Donnelly, for example, told the committee that

> I don't think you can predict you will not have to introduce ground forces in Kuwait. I think any campaign as it starts out would hope that we could reduce the amount of—the necessity for ground forces. But I don't believe you are ever going to see a scenario where ground forces are not going to have to be used. . . . I am one of those airmen that still believes that the way you know you have won a war is when a soldier stands on the ground with an M-16 in his hand and no one is shooting at him.

General Powell stated the case for combined air-ground operations most eloquently when he told the committee on December 14 that

> The very first political objective set out by the President in early August [was] not to punish, not to retaliate, not to see if he [Saddam] will change his mind, but if in the final analysis, if all forms of pressure fail and an offensive military option is required, the purpose of the option would be to eject the Iraqi Army from

Kuwait. Many experts and others in this town believe that this can be accomplished by surgical air strikes or sustained air campaigns without the use of other forces, particularly not ground forces. The fundamental flaw in such strategies is that it leaves the initiative in Saddam's hands. He makes the decision as to whether or not he feels he has been punished sufficiently so that he has no choice but to withdraw. I hope that such strategies might work. That is the key. They might work, but then again, they might not. It is for that reason that these strategies, in my judgment, are not decisive. They do not go to the heart of our political objective. They are not success-oriented . . . . Another flaw in such limited strategies is that it allows Iraq to concentrate essentially on one threat, an air threat. . . . The decision still remains Saddam Hussein's as to whether or not he will withdraw from Kuwait. It is a strategy that relies solely on one dimension, a strategy hoping to win, not designed to win. . . . We must implement a strategy that seizes the initiative and accomplishes our mission, a strategy designed to win.

Not surprisingly, the U.S. decision in early November to almost double its forces in the Gulf reflect this view—sufficient military forces for a campaign planned by air power enthusiasts were probably at hand in early November.

This debate between advocates of air power and those insisting that ground forces are also necessary appears overdrawn and, to some extent, obscures the reality of how a war in the Persian Gulf is likely to fought. Proponents of the air power school warn against the high casualties likely in a frontal attack against Iraqi defenses. General Powell commented, somewhat caustically, that Pentagon planners were as concerned as anyone about minimizing U.S. casualties and were not "mindless." U.S. forces, he told the committee, would not be matched against Iraqi strengths until "they were no longer strengths."

Air power proponents also worry about the early introduction of U.S. ground forces into the conflict, expressing concern that a "combined" air-ground campaign will involve the immediate and simultaneous application of air and ground power. General Powell interrupted a committee member's question, however, when the member asserted that the JCS chairman was calling for the use of ground and air power "at the same time" with the assertion that "I never said that."

My review of the testimony presented to the committee, as well as private conversations with former and active defense officials, convinces me that we will fight a phased campaign in the Persian Gulf. The war is likely to begin with an air campaign against strategic and military targets in Iraq and then proceed to a sustained air campaign against Iraqi military forces in or near Kuwait. The final phase of the campaign would involve the commitment of ground forces. Advocates of air power will likely get a full opportunity to see if air power can win it by itself. But the U.S. military has made sure that sufficient ground force capability is available to do the job, if air power does not force Iraq's withdrawal from Kuwait.

Phase I—The Strategic Air Campaign

According to testimony before the committee, the first task in a strategic air campaign against Iraq would be to establish air superiority. Iraqi aircraft, airfield, and air defense assets, particularly surface-to-air missiles, would be top priority targets at the outset. Iraq's ballistic missiles would also be targeted from the outset in an effort to preempt any Iraqi attacks against Israel, Saudi Arabia, and other Arab countries.

The air campaign would then focus on Iraq's chemical, biological, and nuclear capabilities—stockpiles, delivery vehicles, production facilities, and so on. Iraqi military command and control complexes would be high priority targets as well. The strategic air campaign probably would include Iraq's defense industrial base as well.

Witnesses appearing before the committee expressed little, if any, doubt that coalition air forces could successfully execute the strategic air campaign. Generals Dougherty and Donnelly, in addition to former Assistant Chief of Naval Operations for Air Warfare Admiral Robert Dunn, were confident that air superiority could be established rapidly, perhaps in a day or two. The entire strategic air campaign would take somewhat longer, perhaps a week or so in duration.

The anti-Iraq coalition has between 1,200 and 1,500 aircraft deployed in the Persian Gulf, as well as cruise missiles on ships. Land-based aircraft might be capable of two sorties per day, and sea-based aircraft could mount one sortie per day from carriers in the Indian Ocean and eastern Mediterranean. An estimate of 2,000 daily sorties seems reasonable. Air attrition rates historically average approximately 0.5 percent of sorties flown, but this campaign would be particularly intense during the initial stages. At a daily rate of 2,000 sorties, aircraft losses during the strategic air campaign might average 10 aircraft per day or 70 to 80 during this phase of the war. Total anti-Iraq coalition casualties, the bulk of which would be American, could be expected to be in the low hundreds including fewer than a hundred fatalities.

Combat losses during the strategic air campaign could be higher than these rough estimates. Moreover, the coalitions ability to sustain a 2,000 per day sortie rate for an extended period of time may be reduced due to the distances involved, vagaries of weather, and untested logistical support:

> The distances from a typical Saudi Arabian airfield to Baghdad is about 700 miles. Bomber operations from Diego Garcia would cover 3,600 miles each way. Carrier operations are even more daunting: from the Red Sea, 700 miles, from the Mediterranean, 800 miles, and from the North Arabian Sea, 1,600 miles. Attacking targets in the Kuwaiti Theater of Operations (KTO) with land-based aircraft in Saudi Arabia and the Emirates will require an average sortie is just over 400 statute miles in radius. As a consequence, the air campaign in the Persian Gulf will require extensive aerial refueling.

These difficulties notwithstanding, none of the military experts appearing before the committee questioned our ability to execute successfully the strategic air phase of a military campaign against Iraq.

Phase II—The Tactical Air Campaign

During this phase of the war, air power would be used against Iraqi military forces in the Kuwait theater of operations: operational and tactical reserves in their assembly areas, supply depots, field command headquarters, and first echelon forces deployed in their defensive positions along the border and coast in Kuwait. The objective would be to interdict the highway and rail lines of communication north of Basra, destroy the logistics facilities in southern Iraq, reduce and disrupt Iraqi reserves in the rear areas, and reduce the forward defenses of the Iraqi army.

The limited road and rail network, the large natural lake of the Hawr Al Hammar, and the marshy conditions of the lower Tigris-Euphrates delta constrict available lines of communication from Iraq to its forces in southern Iraq and Kuwait to a relatively narrow area around Basra. A successful interdiction campaign concentrated on that area would effectively cut off Iraqi forces deployed south of Basra and in Kuwait from their support.

Iraqi forces in their prepared positions in the desert will be readily identifiable to observation from the air and vulnerable to air strikes. There is some question, however, as to how effective air strikes will be against skillfully dug-in Iraqi troops and armor. Although the Iraqis have little ability to "conceal" their forces from air attack, their ability to provide "cover" from ground attacks—for example, by digging revetments in which tanks can be concealed—will reduce their vulnerability to air attacks. Air attacks against tanks in the open and on the move are far more lethal than attempts to kill each tank individually.

During this phase of the air campaign, it should be possible to generate more sorties because the nominal combat radius required to reach most targets in Kuwait is much shorter than for Iraq. Although air superiority will have been established during the strategic air campaign, the threat from shoulder-fired missiles and anti-aircraft artillery will probably remain formidable. This may require aircraft to attack from high altitude, thus degrading accuracy and effectiveness, or accept increased losses.

Estimating how long or costly this phase of the air campaign is difficult. The attrition rate might be relatively constant—70 to 80 aircraft per week at a 2,000 per day sortie rate—but it could go higher if Iraqi ground forces are less vulnerable to air attacks from medium-to-high altitudes than many military analysts suspect. Over the course of two or three weeks, Colonel Dupuy estimated casualties the entire air campaign would total 1,800 including about 300 fatalities.

There is little doubt that a tactical air campaign against Iraqi forces would inflict heavy losses on Iraq's logistics infrastructure and to its reserves. Iraq's ability to sustain forces deployed in southern Iraq and Kuwait would be weakened and the capability of its operational and tactical reserves reduced. How much damage would be inflicted upon the first echelon forces, whose extensive preparations against a possible ground attack would reduce their vulnerability to direct air attacks, is uncertain. As discussed earlier, the ability of the Iraqi army to withstand a sustained air campaign is at the heart of the dispute between air power proponents and those who challenge the ability of air power to carry the day on its own.

Phase III—The Ground Campaign

The objective of a coalition ground force campaign against Iraqi forces would be their defeat and forcible ejection from Kuwait. Retired senior military officers and military analysts who appeared before the committee emphasized that the key to accomplishing the campaign relatively quickly and with relatively low casualties would be the use of coalition firepower and maneuver:

- The success of the ground phase of an air-land campaign would depend upon the efficacy of air power. General Dougherty told the committee that the "only way to avoid numerous casualties at the outset of conflict in this area is to exploit initially the special strength of our external mobile air forces—air force, army, navy, and marines. It requires the combined efforts of all elements of war fighting—land, sea and air—to force a final resolution."
- Following a massive aerial bombardment of Iraqi forward positions and tactical reserves and extensive artillery preparation, anti-Iraq coalition ground forces would attack to fix Iraqi forces in place in their prepared positions, penetrating and enveloping those positions by ground, airmobile, and amphibious maneuvers.
- In the final stage of the ground campaign, coalition forces would continue a combined air and land attack to destroy Iraqi tactical and operational reserves and trap remaining Iraqi forces in Kuwait.

The three principal variants of the ground campaign were discussed before the committee by Colonel Trevor Dupuy and James Blackwell from the Center for Strategic and International Studies. A frontal attack was dismissed as extremely unlikely—as General Powell remarked, it would be "mindless" to fight a modern war in this manner.

Coalition ground forces are likely to mount shallow and deep envelopment attacks to counter Iraq's defensive strategy, which was so successful against the frontal, human wave attacks of the Iranian army. Attacks against the first echelon forces and the threat of amphibious attacks from the east are intended to hold the forward-deployed forces in their place. The primary purpose of the mobile attack is to destroy Iraq's operational and strategic reserves, particularly the Republican Guard forces along the Kuwaiti border. The success of this ground campaign would depend in large part on the use of air power to attack Iraqi reserves as they moved forward to counter the coalition force. Major armor battles, however, could be involved.

The military experts appearing before the committee agreed that a successful ground campaign could be executed with the forces available to the anti-Iraq coalition after the current buildup is completed. Casualty estimates, however, varied widely depending upon the tactics to be employed, the effectiveness of coalition air forces, and the will of the Iraqi forces to fight. Harvard University military analyst Barry Posen, after noting that unnamed Pentagon sources had told the *New York Times* that U.S. casualties would be in the 10,000 to 20,000 range, was considerably more optimistic:

> Given command of the air by the coalition, and some combination of surprise, skill, and luck, the campaign could conceivably go as well as the Israeli campaign in 1967—which would suggest "low" U.S. casualties—with less than 1,000 dead and 3-4,000 wounded.

Colonel Trevor Dupuy gave the most precise estimates for how costly a war against Iraq might be and how long it might last. Based on his evaluation of the forces on both sides and the possible operations and tactics that might be employed, Colonel Dupuys casualty estimates were as follows:

- 1,800, including 300 dead, for a sustained strategic and tactical air campaign;
- 9,000, including 1,500 dead, for a combined air–land campaign which sought to envelop Iraqi defensive positions in Kuwait;
- 18,000, including 3,000 dead, in the case of a combined air–land campaign that was essentially a frontal attack into the teeth of the Iraqi defensive positions in Kuwait.

Colonel Dupuy estimated that a campaign that would probe for weak spots and then seek to envelop Iraqi positions in Kuwait would last about 33 days, while a campaign that bulled its way through Iraqi defenses might take only 15 days, albeit with higher casualties.

Those appearing before the committee with Colonel Dupuy generally supported his estimates, noting that his predictions on casualty rates prior to Operation Just Cause had been extremely accurate. Several witnesses commented, however, that these estimates were quite speculative. Even those who suspected that casualty rates might be much higher, however, did not question the prospects for eventual success.

Military Outcome

The potential impact of a war in the Persian Gulf, of course, depends on the nature of the war itself—the circumstances under which it is fought, the extent of the damage to the warring parties, and its duration. Analytically, there are three principal scenarios for the outcome of military conflict in the Gulf:

- A "Bloodless" Victory. Air power enthusiasts are vindicated as either Saddam Hussein or a new regime sues for peace and withdraws forces from Iraq. Iraq's nuclear, biological, and chemical capabilities, as well as its air force and air defense assets, are much reduced, but the army survives largely intact. Iraqi casualties and collateral damage are moderate. U.S. casualties are very light.
- A Rapid Victory. A sustained air campaign, first against strategic targets in Iraq and then against Iraqi forces in the Kuwaiti Theater of Operations, is successful and anti-Iraq coalition ground forces retake Kuwait in less than a month with little or moderate resistance from the Iraqi army. Iraqi casualties are high and collateral damage is heavy. U.S. casualties are light to moderate, perhaps 3,000 to 5,000 including 500 to 1,000 or so fatalities.
- A "Bloody" Victory. The sustained air campaign against the Iraqi army fails to destroy the ability of Iraq's army to fight. It takes several months for the coalition ground forces to drive the Iraqi army out of Kuwait. Iraqi casualties are high and collateral damage is heavy. U.S. casualties are heavy, perhaps 10,000 to 20,000 including several thousand fatalities.

Advantages and Risks of Relying on Military Force

In assessing our military options for resolving the crisis in the Persian Gulf, it is necessary to examine more than the military costs and risks. A war in the Persian Gulf, which, as former Ambassador to Israel Samuel Lewis observed, would be the first Arab–American war ever, would have profound consequences in the region, throughout the world, and in the United States. In fact, avoiding the high costs, loss of life, and uncertain implications of war is one of the principal advantages of relying primarily on sanctions or diplomacy for ending the crisis.

Calculating what the impact of a war in the Gulf would be is even more speculative than the task of assessing our military options. But it is critical that we reach judgments about what the political consequences of a war might be and their implications for U.S. interests. The United States may have no other choice than to use force to achieve its objectives in the Persian Gulf because sanctions and diplomacy failed to do the job. It could be, however, that the costs and risks of a war in the Gulf are too great. Each of us must address this basic "threshold" question: if peaceful means cannot persuade Saddam Hussein to withdraw from Kuwait, should we go to war to make Iraq leave?

Advantages

There are six principal advantages of relying on military force to make Iraq comply with the U.N.-approved objectives.

First, unlike sanctions or diplomacy, the use of force does not rely on Saddam's or Iraq's cooperation to achieve the liberation of Kuwait. The Iraqi forces are ejected or flee, having lost the fight. As former Under Secretary Joseph Sisco testified, military force "may prove to be the only way to get [Saddam Hussein] out of Kuwait."

Second, Iraq's capability for mass destruction weapons—chemical, biological and potentially nuclear—and the long-range means to deliver them (missiles and aircraft) will be much reduced. While we (and our allies) may not go to war for the sole purpose of destroying these capabilities, there is little chance that we would go to war without destroying them.

Third, even if the Iraqi army is not heavily damaged, Iraq's ability to wage conventional war, at least in the short term, will be much weaker in the wake of a war. The post-crisis task of containing Iraq will be easier than it would be if the crisis is resolved through sanctions or diplomacy, which would leave Saddam and his military machine intact.

Fourth, Saddam Hussein himself may not survive a war. Several regional experts told the committee that Saddam would likely be replaced by someone else from the Iraqi Baathist party, probably from the military. Saddam's successor, however, would be unlikely to be the risk-taker that Saddam is, even if he shared the same tendencies.

Fifth, as Joseph Sisco observed, a "decisive military victory would vindicate the decision of the moderate Arabs to call for U.S. support and intervention." Our success in defeating Saddam and neutralizing Iraq's military leverage in the region would strengthen the hand of moderate Arab states and give us a strong role in shaping the future regional collective security system.

Finally, the world's access to oil at reasonable prices would be secured in the wake of a war. No longer the regional superpower, Iraq would not be capable of intimidating Saudi Arabia or dominating the regions oil policy.

Risks

There are five principal categories of risk in relying on military force to achieve our objectives in the Persian Gulf. I'll discuss them according to the degree of uncertainty associated with each category of risk, not necessarily the importance or magnitude of the costs being risked.

First, a wave of anti-American terrorism may be set off by a war in the Gulf. In addition to those mounted by Iraqi or Iraqi-backed units, terrorist attacks might be expected from numerous pro-Saddam groups, many of them Palestinian, and from Islamic fundamentalists determined to drive the American infidels out of the Middle East. The absence of terrorist incidents to date reflects Saddam's desire not to provoke a war, not the lack of capability.

How long and intense this anti-American terrorism will last cannot be known. It will certainly last as long as the war does. A war inflicting high costs on the Iraqis is likely to stimulate more terrorist reprisals than one inflicting low costs. A bloodless or rapid victory by the anti-Iraq forces, however, could deflate potential terrorists.

Second, a war in the Gulf could spark increased anti-Americanism among the Arab masses and spur the growth of Islamic fundamentalism. Former Ambassador to Saudi Arabia Herman Eilts observed that U.S. credibility is "not high" because of the "widespread perception of the Arab masses (and of many, perhaps most Arab governments, including those in the anti-Iraq coalition), that the United States is irrevocably pro-Israeli and, as a corollary, anti-Arab, anti-Palestinian and anti-Islamic." He told the committee that

> Among Arab and non-Arab Islamic fundamentalists, the huge U.S. military deployment to Saudi Arabia and its use against Iraq, if this takes place, will be cast as the latest intrusion of Western "Crusaderism," a term that Islamic fundamentalists apply to virtually all forms of Western modernization. Islamic fundamentalism will be strengthened in all Arab states. Saddam Hussein, as reprehensible as he has been, will come to be cast by many Arab and non-Arab Islamists as a martyr.

The rise of anti-American public sentiment throughout the Middle East in the wake of a war seems inescapable.

The extent of Arab participation in a war against Iraq could affect how intense and widespread this public reaction would be. Samuel Lewis noted that it would be worse if only the United States and Great Britain attacked Iraq, but all of the regional experts the committee asked to assess the political impact of a war—Herman Eilts, Samuel Lewis, and former Assistant Secretary of State for Middle Eastern Affairs Richard Murphy—believe that the war would be viewed in the region as an Arab-American one, despite the UN authorization or the participation of several Arab states. As Richard Murphy noted, we provide over 80 percent of the offensive combat force and we built the international consensus against Iraq. It is not surprising that it come across in the region as "an American-led affair."

Joseph Sisco, however, argues that the view that our use of force would produce enduring Arab enmity toward the United States and enhance the influence of regimes hostile to U.S. interests has "some substance" but is "overdrawn":

> Power attracts and power repels. There would be Arab states and other coalition partners fighting on the front line. Force would be applied collectively, which should ameliorate some anti-Americanism. The moderate Arabs would have triumphed. A tidal wave of radicalism taking over in the region is not likely. Egypt at the center of power can assure its survival against internal forces, and Saudi Arabia has proved not to be an easy prey.

Richard Murphy also told the committee that

> It is a common slur to assert that "Arabs only understand force." The reality is that although they have repeatedly miscalculated their position vis-à-vis Israel in the post WWII period, Arab leaders are not suicidal. They respect firmness and consistency in other powers. They understand the abiding American support for Israel's security, respect Israeli military capabilities and have increasingly come to terms with the need to accommodate themselves to the existence of Israel.

If we successfully use force to oust Saddam from Kuwait, we may win increased respect and standing in the region, but it will be accompanied by greater public animosity. It is unlikely, however, that, as former Under Secretary of State George Ball claimed, a war in the Gulf would "leave the United States in the position of a pariah in the whole Middle East with not a single friend except Israel."

Third, a war in the Persian Gulf risks greater political instability in the Middle East. The inevitable surge in Palestinian activity stemming from a war would be destabilizing in Jordan. Herman Eilts testified that

King Hussein has lost much prestige in the Arab world and in the West by the position he has taken. In a war situation, it may be expected that the Palestinian component of the Jordanian population [now about 60 percent of the total] will be up in arms against the United States and its allies . . . . Paradoxically, he [King Hussein] had probably never been more popular at home before than he is now, but this is largely because he is following populist sentiment rather than seeking to mold it. Yet Jordan is suffering badly in an economic sense from the crisis and will suffer even more so in the wake of the conflict. It will indeed require foreign assistance to bail it out, or indeed even to keep it going. One cannot exclude the possibility that a military conflict might cause the Jordanian monarch to lose his throne.

Richard Murphy agreed that Jordan would be most vulnerable in the event of war, particularly if Israel would react to Palestinian uprisings by expelling masses of Palestinians into Jordan. Samuel Lewis, however, believed that it depends on how long the war lasted and how bloody it is: "A lengthy war, a matter of months, would certainly produce a lot of pressure . . . on moderate Arab governments, in particular the ones that were allied with us." He also noted that "it has been quite a while since there has been a change of government in the Middle East."

Fourth, a war risks creating an unstable balance of power in the Persian Gulf. Of course, Iraq's seizure of Kuwait reflected an unstable balance—Iraq emerged as the regional superpower after the Iran–Iraq War and was not deterred by Saudi Arabia, Syria, Egypt, or Iran, much less the prospect of U.S. intervention. Virtually all of the regional experts appearing before the committee expressed concern over the impact that a war against Iraq could have upon the regional power balance because the destruction of Iraq's military machine could lead to the disintegration or dismemberment of the Iraqi state. Herman Eilts warned that war would

adversely affect the immediate and the long-term balance of power in the Gulf and Fertile Crescent areas. It will encourage Iran to move into the Shii areas of southern Iraq, Syria to move into the central areas, and Turkey to seek to recover Mosul province. The state of Iraq, politically difficult though it has often been, has to some extent been a balancing element against Iranian westward expansion and Syrian eastward expansion.

It has also been a barrier against past Iranian efforts to export revolutionary Islamic anti-American fundamentalism into the Middle East area.

Former Ambassador to Saudi Arabia James Akins believes that we face an "exquisitely delicate task" in waging war against Saddam Hussein: "How can we destroy Iraq just enough so that it is no longer a threat to the weakest of its neighbors while it remains strong enough to frustrate the expansionist tendencies of the most powerful of these neighbors?"

While all agree that a stable balance of power in the Persian Gulf serves our interests, few are sanguine about our ability to achieve one. For both realpolitik and emotional reasons, the United States tilted toward Iraq during the Iran–Iraq War, which ended with the devastation of Iran's military capability. Our failure to "tilt back" against the new regional superpower undoubtedly contributed to Saddam Hussein's calculation that he could seize Kuwait and get away with it. Joseph Sisco, however, believes that prospects for stability in the Gulf have improved considerably with the end of the cold war because

> nations in the area can no longer play off Washington against Moscow and vice versa. There can develop, therefore, despite the indigenous uncertainties, fragility of regimes and radical trends of fundamentalism, an opportunity to bring about balance and stability in the gulf in the aftermath of the current crisis. I say balance and stability, not peace, because the area will continue to be marked by shifting sands, shifting alliances, conflicting ambitions and national interests, ongoing enmities, and few permanent alignments.

Nevertheless, he too cautions against excessive expectations about what we can achieve in the Gulf. He argues, convincingly I believe, that "we must understand the limits of what we can bring about, that neither peaceful means nor force can achieve a comprehensive settlement, only a new balance of power whose permanence cannot be assured."

Finally, a war in the Persian Gulf would have uncertain implications for the Arab–Israeli peace process. All of the regional experts appearing before the committee agreed that after the crisis is resolved, regardless of whether by sanctions, war, or diplomacy, the Arabs, Europeans, and Soviets will put great pressure on the United States and Israel to revive the now-stagnant peace process. Many experts argued that a successful resolution of the Persian Gulf crisis, which would strengthen moderate Arab states, weaken the radical ones, and demonstrate the power of U.S.-Soviet cooperation, would improve the prospects for settling the complicated Arab–Israeli–Palestinian problem. They also expressed little doubt that a "Saddam win" in the crisis would set back the process, making both Israelis and Palestinians alike even less willing to make compromises.

The impact that a solution to the crisis achieved through war would have upon the post-crisis prospects for an Arab–Israeli settlement is debatable. Samuel Lewis, noting the "role of war as midwife historically for peace-making," argued that the peace process "might work better" after a short war because the Israelis would "be a lot more comfortable about going into risks if Saddam Hussein isn't there." He also believed that if the crisis was resolved successfully by political means and Saddam Hussein was "effectively contained and diminished," it would also be a "good platform" for launching the peace process.

Hermann Eilts, on the other hand, was far more pessimistic about the impact of a war in the Persian Gulf on Arab–Israeli settlement prospects:

> Palestinian sentiments will have been aroused even more by what will be seen as a U.S. military action against Iraq. Since Iraq never controlled the Palestinians, its military defeat will hardly affect the PLO leadership. The latter . . . has already showed signs of losing control over the intifada and, in a post-crisis situation, there will be increasing violence and counterviolence in the West Bank and Gaza and in Jerusalem. Sooner or later, the Israeli authorities will seek to "transfer" as many West Bank and Gaza Palestinians as possible to Jordan. . . . Palestinian terrorism against United States and friendly Arab targets will intensify.

Despite wide differences over how a war in the Gulf would affect the prospects for an end to the Arab–Israeli conflict, most of the regional experts appearing before the committee argued strongly that the United States, after a solution to the Gulf crisis achieved by war, would have to revive the peace process. In the words of Richard Murphy:

> As I have said, the war will be viewed in the Arab world as basically one between Iraqis and Americans. Those regimes which have sent troops to Saudi Arabia and support our presence there will be accused of having helped the "leader of the Imperialist Zionist conspiracy" destroy a fellow Arab. To the extent the war stimulates

Arab nationalist sentiments critical of the United States, the pressure on those allies will increase. The consequences to our other interests of such an accusation gaining currency are unpredictable if only because there has never been an Arab–American war. How we move post-war to energize the Arab–Israeli peace process would be key in giving the lie to predictable radical Arab propaganda that Baghdad suffered because only it was serious about a just and durable solution to the region.

Impact of a War Solution on U.S. Interests

As I have stated previously in my White Papers on sanctions and diplomacy, no course of action is likely to secure all our interests in the Persian Gulf today. We must weigh the advantages, costs, and risks of each of our avenues for resolving the crisis—sanctions, diplomacy, and war—to make our final judgments on what we should do in the Persian Gulf.

The principal test for whether a solution to the crisis is acceptable, from our perspective, is the extent of compliance with the UN goals—Iraq's unconditional withdrawal from Kuwait and the restoration of the legitimate government. A solution arrived at through war would accomplish this and address our interest in ensuring that aggression does not pay.

Achieving security and stability in the region requires neutralizing Iraq's military leverage, both its million-man army and its growing capability for mass destruction weapons. A sanctions or diplomatic solution does not address this, leaving the problem of how to contain Saddam Hussein's military machine to the future. A war solution, how-ever, would weaken Iraq militarily and could lead to Saddam's ouster.

But, a weaker, Saddam-less Iraq, as we have seen, does not necessarily mean security and stability in the Gulf. The region has always been plagued by political instability and that is unlikely to change. Nevertheless, a Saddam-led Iraq is a proven quantity—a rogue power that cannot be contained by others in region—and the task of achieving security and stability in the Gulf is likely to be less difficult in the wake of war than after a crisis solution arrived at by sanctions or diplomacy.

Although a war solution may achieve more of our objectives than either sanctions and diplomacy, it is by far the most costly and risky option at our disposal for resolving the Gulf crisis. As I mentioned earlier, the principal advantage of peaceful solutions is that they avoid a war with its high costs, loss of life, and uncertain implications for U.S. interests. One should turn to war only as a last resort, certain that other means for ending the crisis either will not work or have been exhausted.

In addressing the "threshold" question that I posed earlier—namely, "If peaceful means cannot persuade Saddam Hussein to withdraw from Kuwait, should we go to war to make Iraq leave?"—each of us must consider what the consequences of our "losing" the crisis would be. At a recent conference at the National Defense University, according to Samuel Lewis, the conference participants concluded that a diplomatic solution that gave Saddam a victory would be "disastrous" for U.S. interests in the region because our Arab allies would have to accommodate Saddam Hussein. Victory would undermine the ability of the collective security mechanism in the United Nations to deal with the myriad of regional conflicts certain to emerge in the post-cold war era.

The NDU conferees also concluded that the only worse outcome for the United States would be a long, drawn-out war. I think most would agree that this is the worst case. Thus, deciding whether we should go to war in the Persian Gulf, assuming that other means for resolving the crisis are not available, requires two judgments: first, on the likely costs, risks, and implications of war, and, second, on whether our interests at stake in the Persian Gulf justify going to war.

Conclusions

In this paper, I have attempted to review our principal military options in the Persian Gulf and analyze the costs, risks, and implications of going to war in the Persian Gulf. This report follows my earlier White Papers on sanctions and diplomacy, published respectively on December 21 and December 28, and concludes my examination of the our principal avenues for resolving the crisis—sanctions, diplomacy, or war.

My review of the testimony presented to the committee and other available evidence has led me to draw several conclusions with respect to the military option:

On How a War Might Be Conducted

First, I believe that our military objectives drawn up for a war against Iraq are well defined and limited. Our forces would attack strategic and military targets in Iraq and seek to push Iraqi forces out of Kuwait. It would not be a war to punish the Iraqi people or seize Iraqi territory.

Second, I believe the debate between air power proponents and those insisting that ground forces will be necessary to liberate Kuwait misses the point. I am convinced that if we must go to war, we will fight a phased campaign, one that begins with an air campaign against strategic and military targets in Iraq, then proceeds to a sustained air campaign against Iraqi military forces in or near Kuwait, and ends with the commitment of ground troops. Advocates of air power will likely get a full opportunity to see if air power alone can win the war, but there appears to be sufficient ground force capability available to finish the job if necessary.

Third, while I believe the possibility of achieving a "bloodless victory" is small, the prospects for a rapid victory with light to moderate American casualties, perhaps 3,000 to 5,000 including 500 to 1,000 or so fatalities, are high. I judge the risk of a bloody campaign, with casualties in the 10,000 to 20,000 range including several thousand fatalities, to be small.

Fourth, I am convinced that we do not face another Vietnam in the Persian Gulf. There are four principal reasons why there is little risk of a long, drawn-out war:

- A war in the Gulf would not be fought in the jungle, but in the desert, where there is little cover and concealment for Iraqi forces.
- There are no friendly countries around Iraq, and we would not have to worry about any Cambodian sanctuaries or Ho Chi Minh trails.
- We would not be fighting a guerrilla force supported by a sympathetic population, but a uniformed military that has occupied and largely depopulated Kuwait.
- In Vietnam, our military forces were constrained by policies of gradualism and concern about escalating the war to bring in the Soviet Union or China; these constraints will not apply in the Persian Gulf.

On Issues Affecting Our Ability to Fight a War

Fifth, while I believe our forces in the Gulf may not reach their peak readiness for combat operations until early February, when the most newly arrived ground units will have had time to acclimate, most of our forces will be ready by January 15. U.S. Air Force and U.S. Navy units will be fully available and ready, as will a large number of our ground combat forces.

Sixth, in the event of a war, I am confident that most, if not all, of our principal allies will join our forces in the air campaign against Iraq and the air–land campaign against the Iraqi forces occupying Kuwait. In particular, I believe that Arab forces are willing to engage Iraqi forces in Kuwait and that we should plan accordingly.

Seventh, I believe that while Saddam Hussein probably will attempt to break up the wartime coalition against him by attacking Israel, his effort will fail. Israel is likely to respond briefly and in kind, and our Arab allies are likely to keep on fighting Iraq.

On the Post-Crisis Implications of a War

Eighth, I believe that the political risks of a war in the Persian Gulf probably exceed the military risks. The long-term implications in the region and for U.S. interests are uncertain, and we must turn to the military option only as a last resort.

On the Bottom Line

Finally, I believe that the interests we have at stake in the Persian Gulf are vital. If all else fails, they are worth going to war for. Our abhorrence of war and concern about its risks must not deter us from securing vital interests. On a vote to authorize the president to use force to liberate Kuwait, the right vote is "yes."

Appendix A
Compensation for Front-Line Regimes

It is reasonable to expect that continued maintenance of the coalition would require substantial financial flows from the rich nations and those benefiting from the current high oil prices to those countries such as Egypt, Turkey, and Jordan that have been most affected by the decline in remittances from and trade with Kuwait and Iraq.

Egypt, for example, will probably lose several billion dollars in revenues over a year's time. This would include losses from a now-prostrate tourist business, from the decline in Suez Canal revenues due to the embargo, and about $1 billion a year in hard currency remittances to Egyptian workers who have left Iraq and Kuwait and are being dumped into the already beleaguered Egyptian economy, becoming part of Egypt's pressing social problems rather than part of their solution. These costs are in addition to those incurred by providing about 30,000 ground troops to the multinational military force in Saudi Arabia.

Turkey promptly shut down the oil pipeline that runs from Iraq through Turkey to the Mediterranean Sea, closing off an important export avenue for Iraqi oil, along with about 70 percent of Turkey's own oil supply. Also, Iraq has reportedly impounded about $1.5 billion in Turkish assets. The Turkish minister of information estimates it will lose about $8 billion a year, from a total Turkish economy of about $100 billion.

The Jordanian economy is being devastated by the crisis, more so than any other country. Prior to the invasion, it was tied inextricably to the economies of Iraq and Kuwait. Iraq and Kuwait bought about a third of Jordan's total exports, including more than two thirds of its industrial output. The IMF recently estimated that Jordan stands to lose about 55 percent of its GNP over a year's time as a result of the embargo. This loss occurs throughout the economy and is difficult to replace simply through an input of dollars into the national treasury. Jordan is also shouldering the heavy burden of a substantial tide of refugees from Iraq and Kuwait. The inevitable result will be social dislocation, unemployment, and political combustibility.

In addition to this economic crisis, King Hussein of Jordan faces serious political pressures stemming primarily from the fact that the majority of his country's population is Palestinian and supportive of Saddam Hussein as a strong Arab leader committed to the future of a Palestinian homeland. Despite these economic and political pressures, Jordan's trade with Iraq is down to a trickle.

Substantial funds have been pledged by the international community in relief of the "front-line" states suffering most from the crisis. Administration reports are that almost $13.5 billion have been pledged in this cause, of which about $10.8 billion are earmarked for Egypt, Turkey, and Jordan. The Administration is reportedly seeking additional such contributions of $4 billion to $5 billion from the Persian Gulf states.

Additional revenues produced by higher oil prices make it easier for our Persian Gulf allies to contribute to this effort. It is estimated, for example, that Saudi Arabia enjoys extra profits of some $150 million a day, assuming an oil price of $32 per barrel. At that rate, the current Saudi pledge to front-line states represents only about four to five weeks of extra profits. Therefore, the administration goal of marshaling $4 billion to $5 billion more in relief for the hardest-hit countries should not be difficult to achieve.

Appendix B
Hearings and Consultations with Experts

In addition to materials in the public domain and informal consultation with recognized experts, this report is based on five hearings the committee held on December 12, 13, 14, and 17, 1990. The hearings were focused as follows:

Sustaining the U.S. Buildup and Maintaining a Viable Military Threat considered the U.S. ability to provide logistics support for the forces deployed in the Persian Gulf and to sustain the current buildup of forces without a degradation in the readiness of the force. On December 12 the committee heard from:

> *General Edward C. Meyer,* USA (Ret.), chief of staff of the army from 1979 to 1983.

> *Dr. Larry Korb,* The Brookings Institution, former assistant secretary of defense for manpower, reserve affairs, and logistics.

> *General Duane H. Cassidy,* USAF (Ret.), commander, U.S. Transportation Command from 1987 to 1989, and former air force deputy chief of staff for personnel.

Military Conflict in the Persian Gulf and its Consequences—The Air Campaign discussed the potential for achieving U.S. and UN objectives in the Persian Gulf through an air war only and the costs and uncertainties inherent in such a campaign. During the morning of December 13 the committee heard from:

> *Dr. Eliot Cohen,* professor and director of strategic studies for the Paul H. Nitze School of Advanced International Studies, The Johns Hopkins University.

General Charles L. Donnelly Jr., USAF (Ret.), former commander in chief, U.S. Air Forces in Europe, and commander, Allied Air Forces Central Europe. General Donelly served two years as chief of the U.S. Military Training Mission in Saudi Arabia.

General Russell E. Dougherty, USAF (Ret.), former commander, Strategic Air Command and the director of U.S. Strategic Target Planning.

Admiral Robert F. Dunn, USN (Ret.), former assistant chief of naval operations (air warfare).

Colonel Trevor N. Dupuy, USA (Ret.), historian and military analyst.

Military Conflict in the Persian Gulf and its Consequences—The Ground-Air Campaign addressed the capability for achieving U.S. and UN objectives in the Persian Gulf through a combined ground-air campaign and the costs and uncertainties inherent in such a campaign. During the afternoon of December 14 the committee heard from:

General William E. DePuy, USA (Ret.), first commander of the U.S. Army Training and Doctrine Command, responsible for the resurgence of air-ground coordination and integrated campaign planning in the army.

General Charles L. Donnelly Jr., USAF (Ret.).

General Frederick J. Kroesen, USA (Ret.), former commander in chief, U.S. Army Europe, and vice chief of staff of the army.

Colonel Harry G. Summers, Jr., military analyst and commentator.

Dr. James A. Blackwell, Jr., military analyst and deputy director of political-military studies at the Center for Strategic and International Studies.

Military Conflict in the Persian Gulf and its Consequences provided an update on the situation in the Persian Gulf and the current status of the buildup of U.S. and coalition forces. On December 14 the committee heard from:

> *Dick Cheney*, secretary of defense.

> *General Colin Powell*, USA, chairman of the Joint Chiefs of Staff.

Post-Crisis Implications of War in the Persian Gulf examined the short-term and long-term consequences of a war in the Middle East for Iraq, for the region, and for the United States. On December 17 the committee heard from:

> *Ambassador Herman Eilts*, currently with the department of international studies, Boston University, where he is professor and director of the Center for International Relations, ambassador to Saudi Arabia (1965–1970) and Egypt (1973–1979).

> *Ambassador Richard Murphy*, senior fellow on the Middle East for the Council on Foreign Relations, former assistant secretary of state for Middle Eastern Affairs, ambassador to Syria (1974–1978) and Saudi Arabia (1981–1983).

> *Ambassador Samuel Lewis*, currently president of the U.S. Institute of Peace, ambassador to Israel (1977–1985).